HAIR, CLOTHING, AND TIRE TRACK EVIDENCE

For Mark, one of the "1817 Oak Street Boys"
and my best man.

Acknowledgments

This book would not have become a reality without the loving support of my wife, Joan. Thanks to Kelly, Courtney, and Danielle Conrad; Jeff Carpenter; Anne and Samantha Scritsmier; Amy Bauman; and Diane Biamonte, who contributed to some of the images. Deep appreciation to Steven Dunn, President, Ken-A-Vision Mfg. Co., Inc., and Dave Doty for the kind loan of a comparison microscope and digital camera equipment. Thanks to Joe Elliot and Mathew Bacon of School Specialty for their support. Thank you to Lawrence Quarino, Ph.D., D-ABC, Director of Forensic Science Program, Cedar Crest College, Allentown, PA, for his careful reading of the manuscript and many helpful comments and suggestions. Special thanks to Ken Rando for helping with the electrons.

Library of Congress Cataloging-in-Publication Data

Rainis, Kenneth G.
    Hair, clothing, and tire track evidence : crime-solving science experiments /
    Kenneth G. Rainis.
      p. cm. — (Forensic science projects)
    Includes bibliographical references and index.
    ISBN 0-7660-2729-5
      1. Criminal investigation—Juvenile literature. 2. Hair—Analysis—Juvenile literature. 3. Fibers—Analysis—Juvenile literature. 4. Evidence, Criminal—Juvenile literature. 5. Forensic sciences—Juvenile literature. I. Title.
    HV8077.5.H34R34 2006
    363.25'62—dc22
                                    2005037399

Printed in the United States of America

10 9 8 7 6 5 4 3 2 1

To Our Readers: We have done our best to make sure all Internet Addresses in this book were active and appropriate when we went to press. However, the author and the publisher have no control over and assume no liability for the material available on those Internet sites or on other Web sites they may link to. Any comments or suggestions can be sent by e-mail to comments@enslow.com or to the address on the back cover.

Every effort has been made to locate all copyright holders of material used in this book. If any errors or omissions have occurred, corrections will be made in future editions of this book.

Illustration Credits: All illustrations by Kenneth G. Rainis, except as follows: © 2006 by Stephen Rountree (www.rountreegraphics.com), pp. 16, 39, 41, 60, 96; © 2006 Jupiterimages Corporation, pp. 14, 18; AP Wide World, pp. 50, 64, 67, 80, 88; Neo/SCI, division of Delta Education, LLC., Nashua, NH, p. 43; Ken-A-Vision Comparison Scope (T-1922). Courtesy of Ken-A-Vision Mfg. Co., Inc., Kansas City, MO, p. 10 (a).

Background Photos: © 2006 Jupiterimages Corporation.

Cover Photos: © 2006 Jupiterimages Corporation (tire tracks and hair); Kenneth G. Rainis (cloth).

HAIR, CLOTHING, AND TIRE TRACK EVIDENCE

Crime-Solving Science Experiments

Kenneth G. Rainis

Science Consultant:
Brian Gestring, M.S.
Director of Forensic Science Program
Pace University
New York, New York

 Enslow Publishers, Inc.
40 Industrial Road
Box 398
Berkeley Heights, NJ 07922
USA
http://www.enslow.com

CONTENTS

● ●

CHAPTER 1

The Case of the Silent Witness

John and Janice Dodson were newlyweds. Married in July 1995, they decided to take a hunting trip to the mountains in western Colorado. Janice was an experienced elk hunter. John had never been hunting before. Coincidentally, Janice's ex-husband, J. C. Lee, would also be in the general area with another hunting party.

On the morning of October 15, a vacationing Texas law enforcement officer heard screams. He had been hunting near the Dodson camp. He ran toward the sound and saw Janice Dodson standing in a field about two hundred yards from the Dodson camp along a fence line. When he reached the camp, he found John Dodson, dead. It looked like a hunting accident— a bullet hole through Dodson's hunting vest. But sometimes things are not what they seem.

The Texas law officer called for help. Sheriff's deputies arrived and took charge of the scene. They supervised the recovery of the body. An autopsy later showed that John Dodson was shot three times. The fatal bullet had gone straight though his chest.

Mesa County sheriff's deputies had collected valuable evidence at the scene: a .308-caliber shell case found about sixty yards from the body. Another identical shell casing was found near the fence line. The case was declared a homicide (the deliberate killing of one person by another).

Deputies interviewed Janice. They noticed that she had mud on the lower part of her hunting overalls and boots. She stated that she had stepped into a bog area (a wet, mossy area). Investigators next turned to J. C. Lee, Janice's ex-husband. He had an alibi (a confirmed account of where he was or what he did). He had been hunting all day with a business associate—miles away. However, he told deputies someone had come into camp and stolen his .308 rifle. They also took a box of .308 cartridges.

Investigators collected three mud samples: one from a pond next to the Dodson camp, one from the cattle pond near the Lee camp, and one from the bog area. These three samples would be compared to the mud on Janice Dodson's boots and clothing. The samples were sent to the Colorado Bureau of Investigation in Denver.

At the lab, forensic scientist Jacqueline Battles analyzed each sample. She made photographs of the microscopic appearance of each sample. In her written pretrial report to the lab director, she made the following conclusions:

- the dried mud on Janice Dodson's boots and clothing was consistent with the mud at the cattle pond near the Lee camp. Both samples contained bentonite (a water-absorbent clay).

- The dried mud on Dodson's clothing and boots was not consistent with mud from the other two collection sites—the bog or the pond near the Dodson campsite. These two samples did not contain bentonite.

Forensically, the trace evidence placed Janice Dodson in the Lee camp around the time that his .308 rifle was stolen. The murder weapon was never found.

District Attorney Frank Daniels had nothing but circumstantial evidence to present at Janice Dodson's trial. Such evidence indirectly points to someone's guilt but does not prove it. Daniels told the jury that Janice Dodson's motive was to inherit John Dodson's estate worth over half a million dollars. The jury convicted Janice Dodson. She is serving a life sentence without parole in a Colorado state prison for women.

Physical Evidence

Every crime leaves a visible sign called physical evidence that can lead a careful investigator back to the perpetrator—the individual who committed the act. The form of physical evidence can be a tire track, an impression in the soil or even snow, a scratch or other marking, or particles and fibers that need to be viewed through a microscope.

Tools You Will Need

You will use this book as a guide in learning how to analyze evidence. Evidence is a material object used to state facts. In this book, we will be taking a closer look at two kinds of evidence:

- **Contact Evidence**—Marks and impressions left behind after something contacts a surface.
- **Trace Evidence**—Fibers, hairs, and particles left behind at the scene, or taken away from the crime scene.

In the process, you will try your hand at solving various mysteries.

All forensic investigators carry a case notebook. You should too. It will help you to collect facts about the cases you are working on and record and organize data. Crime scene investigators also carry a magnifying glass to examine trace and contact evidence. Sometimes higher magnification is required, and a stereomicroscope or compound microscope is used.

In the Dodson Case, investigators used a microscope to compare particle evidence in soil samples. Since the early 1920s, trace evidence analysts have used a special type of microscope, called a comparison microscope. It allows the investigator to view and compare the images of two separate pieces of evidence at the same time (see Figure 1). Many of the hair and fiber comparisons in this book were taken using a comparison microscope.

FIGURE 1.

Magnifying Trace Evidence

(a)

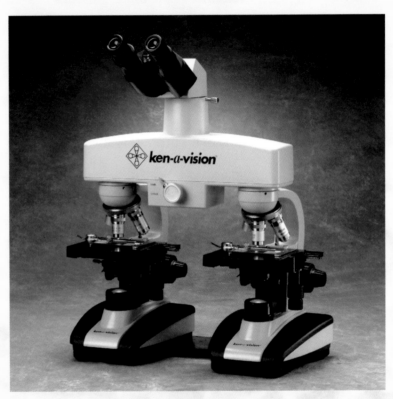

(a) A comparison microscope allows an investigator to look at two images at the same time. It helps them do a side-by-side comparison of two samples.

(b)

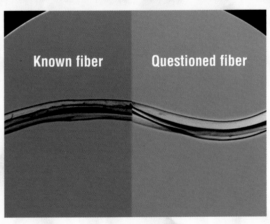

Known fiber   Questioned fiber

400X

(b) A comparison of two carpet fibers as seen under the comparison microscope.

Most of the materials you will need as a trace and contact evidence investigator can be found around the house or in local stores.

The Scientific Method

Sheriff's investigators used an important procedure in the Dodson case: the scientific method. They followed these steps in their analyses: They made a careful guess (a hypothesis) to explain what they observed (e.g, soil-covered boots). They used a method (microscopic analysis) to test their guess, and used their results (data) to conclude whether their guess was correct or whether it should be changed. All forensic scientists use the scientific method to test their ideas and come to a conclusion or finding.

Findings

Forensic scientists must summarize and report their findings (conclusions) to law enforcement authorities and the court. They present formal pretrial reports and verbal testimony.

At times in this book you will be asked to prepare a report to the court. Your pretrial report should contain the following parts and be in this order:

- Observation of data
- Interpretation of data
- Hypothesis
- Testing of hypothesis and procedures followed
- Summary; findings of fact

Your pretrial report should be word processed, typed, or written clearly in blue or black ink. Most trace evidence examiners use photographs to illustrate their findings. They usually present two images—one that has no markings and one that has the points of interest identified.

Keeping Safe as a Junior Trace Evidence Analyst

The most important ingredient for success is safety.

1. Be serious about forensic science. An easygoing attitude can be dangerous to you and to others. Always investigate under the supervision of a knowledgeable adult.

2. Read instructions carefully and completely before beginning any case in this book. Discuss your procedure with a knowledgeable adult before you start. A flaw in your design could cause an accident. *If in doubt, check with a science teacher or other knowledgeable adult.*

3. Keep your work area clean and organized. Never eat or drink anything while conducting investigations.

4. Wear protective goggles when working with chemicals or when performing any other experiment that could lead to eye injury.

5. Do not touch chemicals with your bare hands unless instructed to do so. Do not taste chemicals or chemical solutions. Do not inhale vapors or fumes from any chemical or chemical solution.

6. Clean up any chemical spill immediately. If you spill anything on your skin or clothing, rinse it off immediately with plenty of water. Then report what happened to a responsible adult.

7. Keep flammable liquids away from heat sources.

8. Always wash your hands after conducting experiments. Dispose of contaminated waste or articles properly.

9. Be a responsible Web surfer. Explore only genuine topic areas approved by a responsible adult.

How This Book Is Organized

Chapter 1 of this book gave you a true-life example of how an individual left behind physical signs of her presence at a crime scene. Particle evidence analysis was then able to connect the perpetrator to the crime scene. Chapter 2 gives you important background information about different types of contact and trace evidence analysis. You will learn how such evidence is collected and analyzed to identify an individual or place an individual at a crime scene. You will learn how evidence analysts do their work and report to the court.

In Chapter 3, you can read about actual cases that were solved by examining trace or contact evidence. Learn how forensic science exposed the perpetrator. Each of these cases has a project that will let you develop your forensic skills. It also has recommended science project ideas to practice and expand on what

Impression marks, such as tire tracks, are studied by forensic scientists to gather evidence at a crime scene.

you have learned. You may decide to use one of these ideas as a start to your own science fair project.

In Chapter 4, *Investigating the Crime*, you and your friends will have an opportunity to use your newly acquired trace analysis skills to solve a crime that closely follows an actual event. Like all professional forensic microanalysts, you will need to write a report that provides a clear summary of your analysis results.

Lastly, you can go to Chapter 5 to get explanations for the various questions and cases contained in this book. Let's get to work!

CHAPTER 2
●●●●●●●●●●●●●●●●●●●

Particles, Fibers, and Marks

As you read in Chapter 1, there are different types of trace evidence associated with a crime scene. Two of these types are trace evidence (fibers, hairs, and particles) and contact evidence (marks and impressions). Before you get started with the cases and projects in Chapter 3, let's learn about how forensic scientists study particles, fibers, and marks during an investigation.

Particle Collection and Analysis

Particles are tiny pieces of physical evidence. They can be powders or soil particles. Powders are fine, dry masses of particles. Grinding or crushing materials usually creates powders. Cosmetics and many foods, such as flour and confectioner's sugar, are powders. Soil is a mixture of different-sized and shaped particles— minerals and sands, clay, and organic matter.

Forensic investigators use the tape lift method to collect particle evidence (see Figure 2). Later, the collected evidence can be viewed directly under the microscope, or it can be removed from the tape in the laboratory and studied separately.

FIGURE 2.

Tape Lift Method for Particle Collection

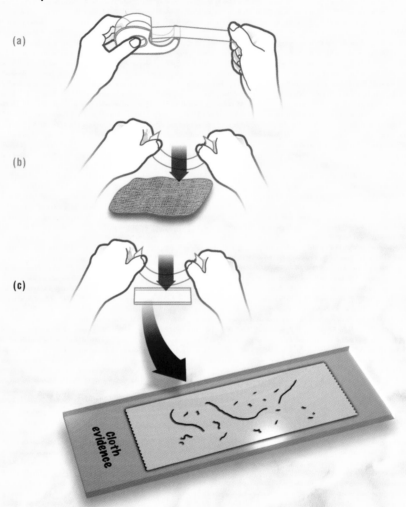

(a) Pull out a 2-inch length of clear sticky tape from a dispenser.

(b) Touch the tape to the surface containing the particles and/or fibers to be collected.

(c) Remove the tape and attach it to a glass microscope slide. Label the slide for later evidence recording.

Marks and Impressions

Forensic investigators usually examine the following types of contact evidence at crime scenes:

- *Broken parts* having irregularly fractured edges
- *Impression marks* on smooth surfaces made by tires, fabrics, or fingers
- *Indented impressions* made on soft surfaces by feet, tires, or objects
- *Contact marks* or scratches left by hard edges scraping or shearing, such as tool marks
- *Striation marks* made by sliding, such as when a screwdriver slides along a surface.

Fibers

The majority of trace evidence analysis deals with fibers. A fiber is the smallest unit of a fabric that has a length many times greater than its diameter. Natural fibers come from plants or animals. For example, a natural animal fiber is silk. Synthetic fibers are man-made from chemicals that are squeezed out through tiny holes under pressure to form threads. An example of a synthetic fiber is polyester. Table 1 is a guide to different types of fibers.

Hairs

A hair is a thread that is made mostly of keratin—a fibrous protein. Like all hair of all mammals, human hair grows from a hair follicle, a porelike organ within

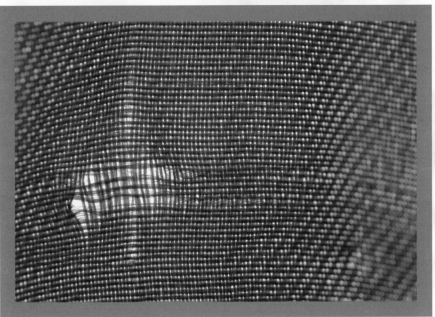

Rope fibers and cloth fibers are types of evidence that can link a suspect to a crime scene.

TABLE 1. Guide To Natural and Synthetic Fibers

TYPE	EXAMPLE	COMMENT
ANIMAL	Wool	FIBER: Cylindrical, coiled USE: Cloth and fabrics; carpets
	Silk cultivated silkworm *Bombyx mori*	FIBER: Filament; nearly triangular USE: Cloth and fabrics
PLANT	Cotton *Gossypium species*	FIBER: Spiral twist USE: Cloth or fabric; thread; twine
	Flax *Linum usitatissimum*	FIBER: Cylindrical, long and hollow USE: Table linens; clothing
SYNTHETIC	Rayon	FIBER: Extruded filament USE: Clothing fabrics (long-filament rayon); filling materials in pillows, mattress pads, quilts; filtering agents in cigarettes (short-filament rayon).
	Nylon	FIBER: Stretched or extruded elastic filament USE: Carpeting
	Polyester	FIBER: Stretched; hollow USE: Lightweight clothing; insulation; water- and wind-resistant fabrics

the skin. Hair is made up of two distinct parts: the shaft, or the portion that projects from the skin, which we see; and the root, which is inside the follicle deep within the skin. Figure 3 shows the structure of human hair and how it grows. In this book, we will concentrate on studying scalp hairs. Scalp hairs grow less than half an inch (13 millimeters) per month. They are made of three distinct layers: cuticle, cortex, and medulla.

CUTICLE

The cuticle is the hard, outside covering of a hair shaft that protects the inner layers. It is made of overlapping scales (see Figure 4). There are three basic scale shape structures that make up a hair cuticle—crown-like (coronal), petal-like (spinous), and flattened (imbricate). Combinations and variations of these types are possible.

Obtain a rather long strand of hair from your head and hold it by the root between your left forefinger and thumb. Gently draw the hair strand from the root to the tip, applying firm pressure, through the forefinger and thumb of your right hand. Now reverse the procedure, drawing the hair strand from tip to root. Which direction offers more resistance? The resistance you feel is due to the presence of overlapping scales with their edges pointing toward the tip. These scales make up the cuticle. Use this touch method to examine other hair types such as dog hair and wool.

FIGURE 3.
●●●●●●●●●●●●●●●

You and Your Hair

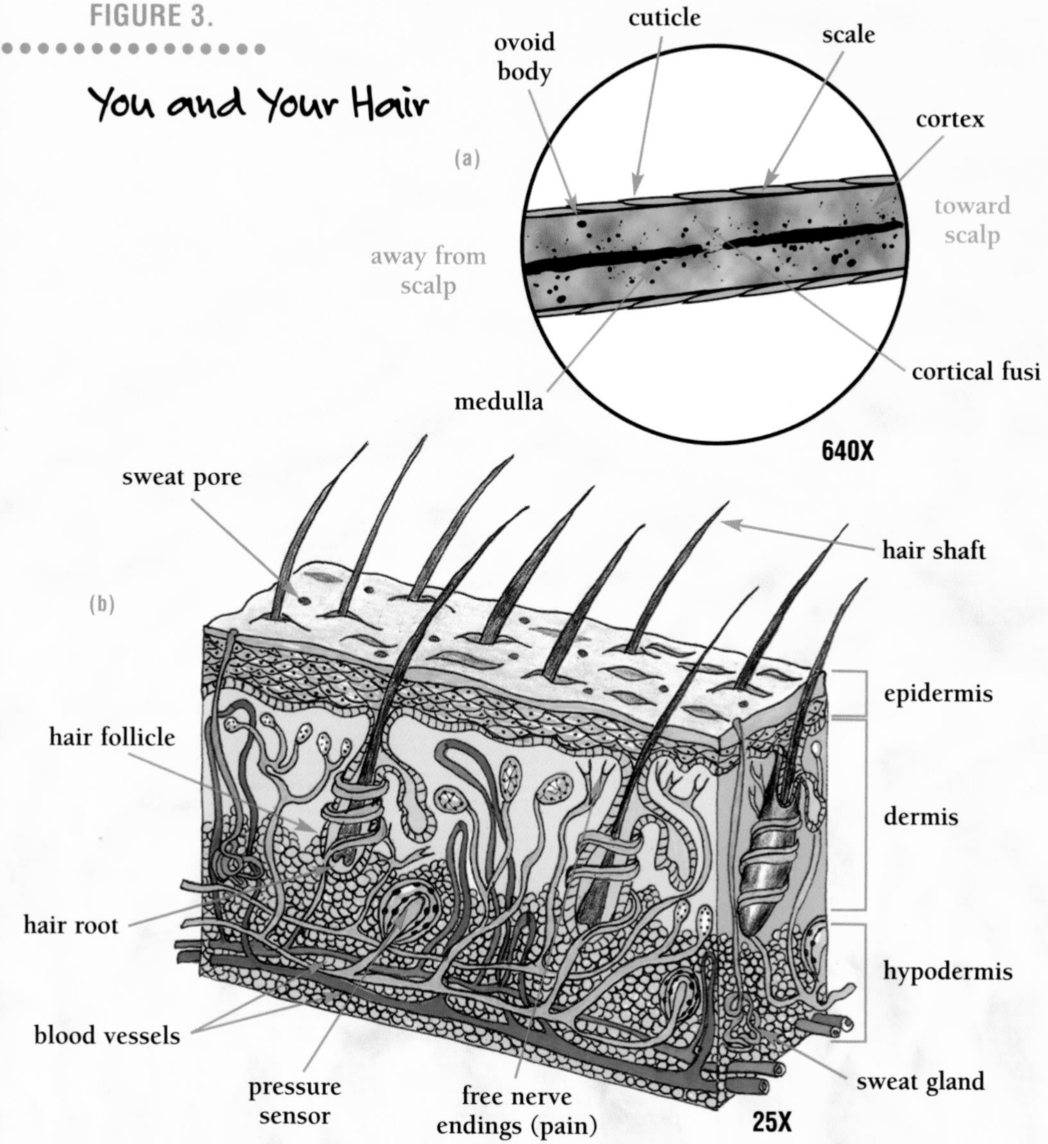

(a)

cuticle

ovoid
body

scale

cortex

toward
scalp

away from
scalp

cortical fusi

medulla

640X

(b)

sweat pore

hair shaft

epidermis

dermis

hair follicle

hair root

hypodermis

blood vessels

sweat gland

pressure
sensor

free nerve
endings (pain)

25X

Hair is made up of two distinct parts: the *shaft*, or the portion that projects from the skin, that we see, and the *root*, which is inside in the follicle deep within the skin.

(a) The parts of a strand of hair.

(b) Cross section of human scalp.

●●●●●●●●●●●●●●●

FIGURE 4.

Cuticle Scales and Scale Imprints

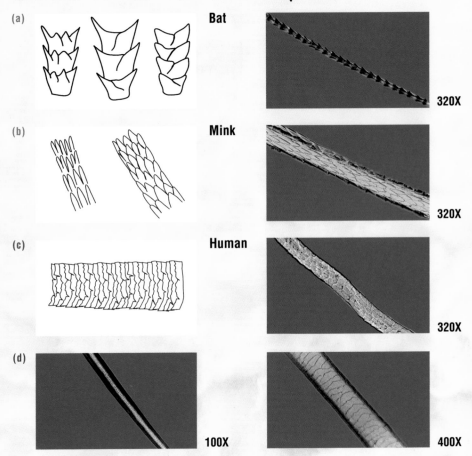

There are three types of cuticle scale types.

(a) Crown-like (coronal) scales are found on bat hair.

(b) Petal-like (spinous) scales are found on rabbit, fox, mink, and raccoon hair.

(c) Flattened (imbricate) scales are found on bear, beaver, cow, horse, deer, and human hair.

(d) These human hair scale imprints were created by placing hair in nail polish on a microscope slide. Before the polish dries, remove the hair and an imprint of the scales remains.

P R O J E C T :

Making Scale Impressions

What You Need:

- an adult
- clear nail polish
- microscope slide
- tweezers
- a hair from your head
- access to a compound microscope

What You Do:

With adult permission, you can microscopically observe a scale pattern by making a scale imprint using clear nail polish. **Caution: Clear nail polish is flammable. Do not use it near an open flame or heat.**

1. With the nail polish brush, paint a one-inch square area in the center of a clean microscope slide.
2. Use tweezers to place a hair in the wet nail polish.
3. Before the polish dries, but after it starts to set, use tweezers to carefully remove the hair.
4. Observe the slide under highest magnification (400–430X) of a compound microscope. (See **Looking at Slides With a Microscope** on page 40 for instructions on using a compound microscope.) Do you see a scale imprint?

You can make scale imprints of various human and animal hairs. Does animal hair look different from human hair?

CORTEX

Most of a human hair shaft (70 to 90 percent) is made of cortex. The cortex may contain pigment granules (that give hair its color) and/or larger bodies that are oval or round, called ovoid bodies. Scientists study the pigment granules and ovoid bodies when examining hair samples.

Pigment granules. Pigment granules contain chemicals called melanins. Melanins give hair its color. There are two kinds of melanin—one colors hair brown to black and one colors hair yellow-blond to red. The amounts of these melanins determine your hair color (see Figure 5). When hair turns gray, a person has stopped making melanin.

A quick way to determine hair color is to observe it under reflected (e.g., room) light while you examine it with a magnifying glass (see Figure 6). Today, it is common for hair to be bleached or dyed. Bleaching removes the pigment and gives hair a yellow tint. Dye can reach either the cuticle or cortex of a hair to change its color (see Figure 7).

Cortical fusi. Cortical fusi are air spaces of different sizes found among the much smaller pigment granules. They are usually found toward the root of human and

FIGURE 5.
●●●●●●●●●●●●●●●

Melanins and Hair Color

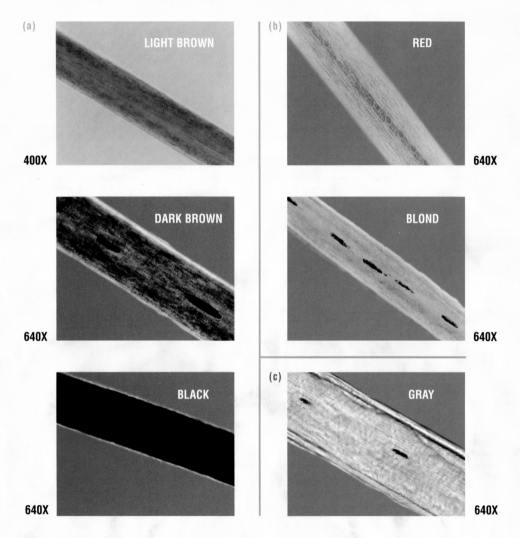

(a) Brown/black pigment granules in light brown, dark brown, and black hair.

(b) Blond/red pigment granules in red and blond hair.

(c) Gray hair shows a loss of pigment granules.

●●●●●●●●●●●●●●

FIGURE 6.

Examining Hair Color

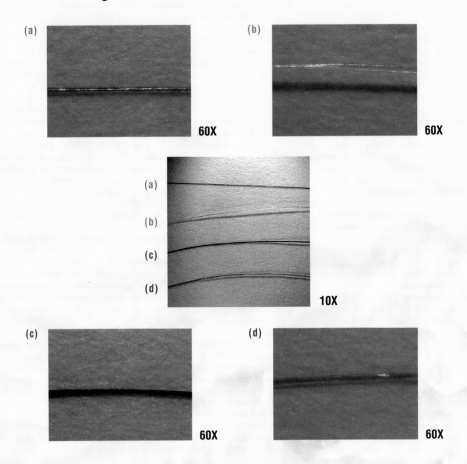

(a) 60X

(b) 60X

(a)
(b)
(c)
(d)

10X

(c) 60X

(d) 60X

Reflected light (light that bounces off a surface) is best for determining hair color. Natural color hair strands are shown, as viewed with a magnifying glass under reflected light:

(a) brown

(b) blond

(c) black

(d) red

FIGURE 7.
●●●●●●●●●●●●

Bleached and Dyed Hair

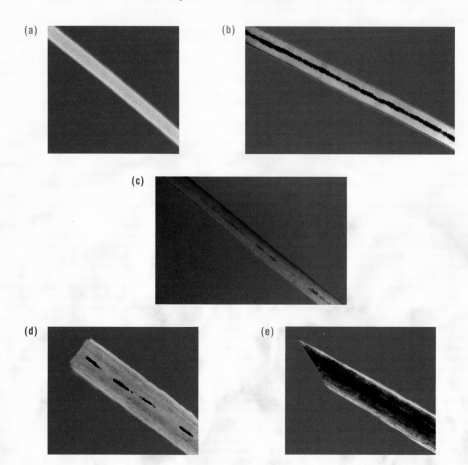

These images show different hair treatments, as seen under a microscope.

(a) bleached hair

(b) highlighted hair

(c) hair dyed red

(d) hair cut with shears

(e) hair cut with a razor

●●●●●●●●●●●●●●

27

animal hairs and may also appear in dyed hair (see Figure 8a).

Ovoid bodies. Ovoid bodies are large round or oval structures. They are common in many animal hairs, especially cattle. Ovoid bodies can also be found in human hair (see Figure 8b).

MEDULLA

The medulla of hair is made up of cells that run through the center of the cortex. Think of it like the lead in a pencil. In humans, this is a small-diameter canal that may be continuous, interrupted, or in some cases, absent. Forensic scientists determine the medullary index of hair. This is a big word, but it simply means the size of the medulla compared to the size of the entire hair shaft. This number is written as a fraction. For example, humans have a medullary value of less than ⅓, or 0.33. That means the width of the medulla is less than ⅓ the width of the entire hair shaft. Animal hair has a medullary index of greater than 0.50. Figure 9 shows how to determine the medullary index. Figure 10 is a guide to animal hair medulla types.

Human hairs can be classified by racial origin: Caucasian (European origin), African (African origin), and Asian (Asian origin). Both African and Caucasian hairs have a medullary core that is either absent or inter-rupted. Hairs of individuals of Asian decent have a continuous medullary core (see Figure 11).

FIGURE 8.

Cortical Fusi and Ovoid Bodies

(a)

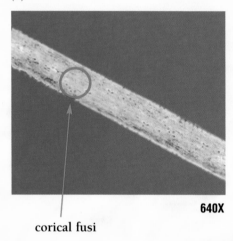

(b)

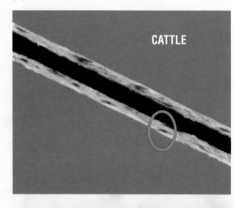

CATTLE

640X

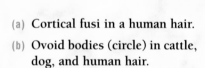

corical fusi

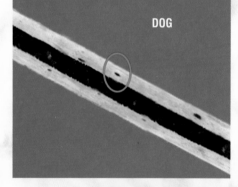

DOG

(a) Cortical fusi in a human hair.

(b) Ovoid bodies (circle) in cattle, dog, and human hair.

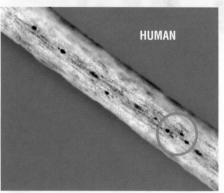

HUMAN

FIGURE 9.
● ● ● ● ● ● ● ● ● ● ● ● ● ● ● ● ●

Determining Medullary Index

(a)

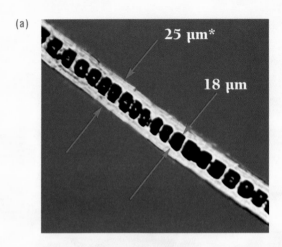

medullary index =

$$\frac{\text{width of medulla}}{\text{width of entire hair}} = \frac{18 \ \mu m}{25 \ \mu m} = 0.72$$

320X

(b)

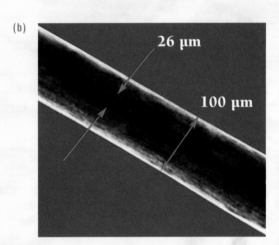

medullary index =

$$\frac{\text{width of medulla}}{\text{width of entire hair}} = \frac{26 \ \mu m}{100 \ \mu m} = 0.26$$

640X

(a) cat hair

(b) human hair

*1 μm = 1 micrometer, which is $\frac{1}{1,000}$ mm.

● ● ● ● ● ● ● ● ● ● ● ● ● ● ● ● ●

FIGURE 10.

Animal Hair Medulla Types

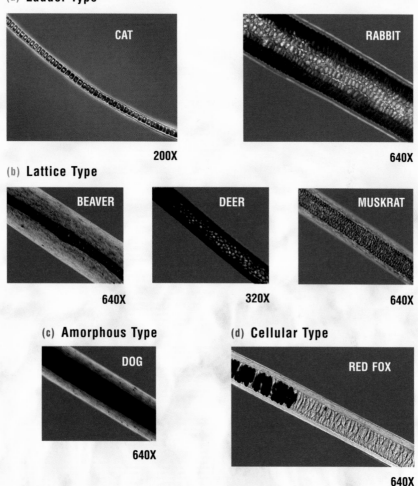

(a) **Ladder Type**

CAT
200X

RABBIT
640X

(b) **Lattice Type**

BEAVER
640X

DEER
320X

MUSKRAT
640X

(c) **Amorphous Type**

DOG
640X

(d) **Cellular Type**

RED FOX
640X

(a) Ladder type: single row (cat); multiple rows (rabbit).

(b) Lattice type: narrow (beaver); wide (deer); aeriform (muskrat).

(c) Amorphous type: dog

(d) Cellular type is found in many animals, such as the red fox.

FIGURE 11.

Human Hair and Racial Origin

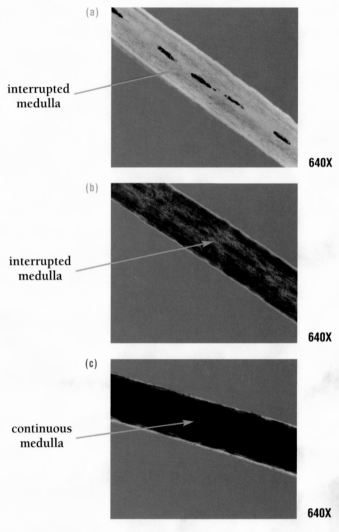

(a) interrupted medulla

640X

(b) interrupted medulla

640X

(c) continuous medulla

640X

(a) Caucasian hair with interrupted medulla.

(b) African hair with absent or interrupted medulla.

(c) Asian hair with continuous medulla.

Hair Roots

The root of human hairs is commonly club-shaped, whereas the roots of animal hairs can differ greatly in appearance (see Figure 12).

Animal Hair Groups

In addition to human hairs, there are three main groups of animal hairs that usually are encountered in forensic cases:

- Deer
- Commercial fur
- Domestic animals

FIGURE 12.

Hair Roots

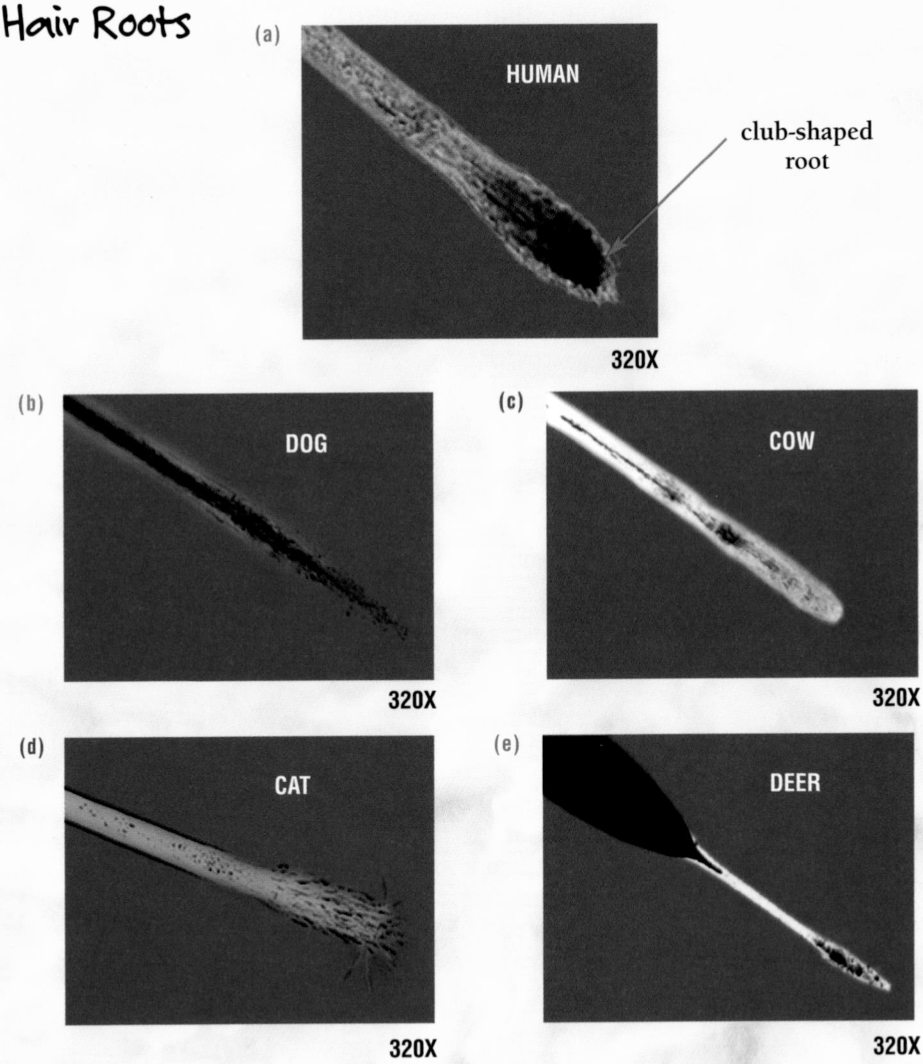

Hair roots of different animals:

(a) human   (d) cat
(b) dog   (e) deer
(c) cow

TABLE 2. Animal Hair Characteristics

ANIMAL	DIAMETER OF HAIR	MEDULLA TYPE	SCALE	COLOR	OVOID BODIES	ROOT
Deer	0.3 mm (300 μm)	wide lattice; spherical cells that occupy entire hair	imbricate—resembles fish scales	varies, in bands along hair shaft	absent	wineglass-shaped
Rabbit	0.8 mm (800 μm)	multiserial; ladder	spinous	varies, bands along hair shaft	absent	elongated
Cat	0.5 mm (500 μm)	uniserial; ladder	spinous	solid	absent	elongated, no distinct shape; fibrils frayed at base of root
Dog	0.75–1.5 mm (750–1,500 μm)	amorphous*	imbricate	solid	present	spade-shaped
Cow	1.0 mm (1,000 μm)	amorphous*	imbricate	solid	many present	elongated
Human	50–150 μm	absent, interrupted, or continuous	imbricate	solid	some present	club-shaped

***Amorphous** means "no pattern."

35

PROJECT:

Making a Hair and Fiber Reference Collection

It is important that you create a reference collection of known examples of hair and fiber types that you can compare against unknown hair and fiber samples. Once you have this reference collection of slides, you can use it to compare slides to unknown fiber samples you collect. These comparisons will be made under the microscope.

What You Need:

- paper bag(s)
- tweezers, fine point
- paper envelope(s)
- permanent black ink marker
- clear sticky tape (3/4-inch)
- index cards, unlined
- hair samples: human, animal
- fabric samples: polyester, cotton, linen, and wool (fabric store)
- plant samples: linen, cotton, and hemp
- magnifying glass
- desk lamp
- light corn syrup
- paper cup
- microscope slides
- medicine dropper

- **plastic coverslips**
- **compound microscope, at least 400–430X magnification**

A forensic hair and fiber examiner recognizes, collects, and preserves physical evidence. These professionals use a number of methods in collecting hair and fiber evidence:

1. Investigators protect clothing or other physical evidence at the crime scene from contamination by placing it in a labeled paper bag for later examination.

2. Investigators collect hair and fiber evidence using tweezers and place the evidence in small paper envelopes. (If an envelope is not available, they fold a sheet of paper and use tweezers to deposit the fiber on the fold in the center of the folded paper. Then they fold the paper lengthwise again and the outer ends in on themselves.) They label the envelope, and then the evidence is transported to the laboratory for examination.

3. Investigators use clear sticky tape to recover fibers from fabrics or other objects. A 2-inch piece of clear tape is carefully placed on top of the fibers to be recovered. Then the tape is removed and immediately attached to a clean glass microscope slide. The slide is placed in a labeled container for transportation to the laboratory.

   Your collection should include as many types of hair and fibers as possible. The following are excellent sources for hair samples: barber, beautician, pet groomer, outdoorsman, and a taxidermist. Fabric stores will usually provide free samples.

Use index cards, or your notebook, to record important information about each known hair and fiber sample, such as date collected; place collected; fiber type (natural—animal/plant, or synthetic); fiber description (microstructure, thickness, length, twist, color, etc.); unique features (unique scales); and measurements of key features such as fiber width.

What You Do:

Evidence Collection

Practice collecting some hairs and fibers, following the techniques just described (see Figure 13). Then you can examine these fibers with a magnifying glass.

Looking at Samples With a Magnifying Glass

A magnifying glass is actually a single-lens microscope. Forensic investigators use the magnifying glass extensively in their work. You should, too. Use tweezers to pick up and examine fibers using a magnifying glass. Use reflected light from a desk lamp to examine fibers against a contrasting background. Such reflected light

FIGURE 13.

Collecting Hair and Fiber Evidence

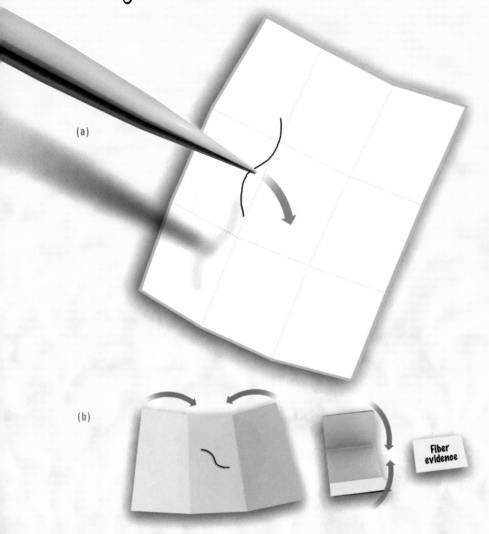

(a)

(b)

(a) Use tweezers to deposit the fiber into an evidence collection envelope or folded paper.

(b) Place the fiber on the fold in the center of the folded paper. Fold the paper lengthwise again and the outer ends in on them. Accurately label the evidence.

examinations, at low magnification, are recommended for accurately determining hair color.

Microscope Slide Preparation

Permanent microscope slide mounts are useful because they are long-lasting slides of dry objects. Use Figure 14 as a guide when making permanent microscope slide preparations.

1. Pour a small amount of light corn syrup into a paper cup.
2. Use tweezers to pick up a fiber from a collection envelope.
3. Place the fiber in the center of a clean microscope slide.
4. Use a medicine dropper to add a single drop of the corn syrup on top of the fiber. (Water can be substituted for light corn syrup, but the preparation will not be permanent.)
5. Place a coverslip over the drop. To avoid air bubbles, slowly lower the coverslip at an angle so that any bubbles will slide off the coverslip and escape.
6. Use a permanent marker to label the slide, usually with a sample and case number.

Looking at Slides With a Microscope

Tape lift preparations (see Figure 2) can be examined directly under a compound microscope. Although this

FIGURE 14.
• • • • • • • • • • • • • •

Making a Permanent Microscope Slide Preparation

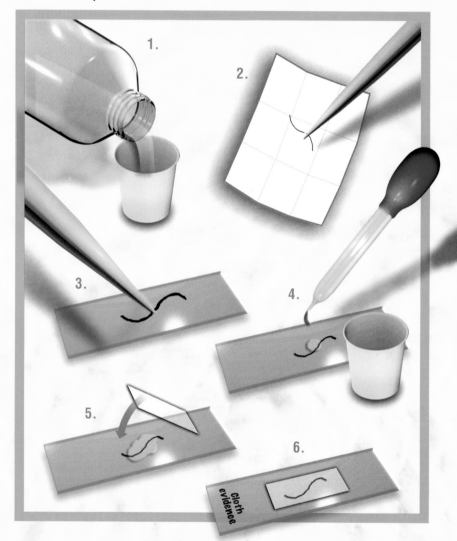

With simple materials, you can make slides of your fiber evidence. Then you can view them under a microscope.

method of mounting a collected hair is the easiest, you may see distortion and a lot of trapped air bubbles. Many times forensic investigators carefully remove the tape from the glass slide, expose the fiber(s), and use tweezers to remove a fiber and make a permanent preparation.

Use Figure 15 as a guide to the parts of a compound microscope as you make the examination of fibers.

1. Position the objective lens in place over the hole in the stage. You should start using the lowest objective magnifying power available. Usually this is 4X. (The total magnification of the image is 4 times the power of the lens in the eyepiece, usually 10. So the total magnification at low power here is $4 \times 10 = 40$.)

2. Use the coarse adjustment knob to raise the 4X objective, from its lowest point, to about 2.5 cm (1 in) from the stage by turning the knob counter-clockwise. This allows room for placing the microscope slide on the stage for viewing.

3. Adjust the mirror or other light source to send light through the fiber. Look through the eyepiece; you should be able to observe an even, bright circle of light.

4. Place the microscope slide containing the fiber to be examined on the stage of the microscope, specimen side up. Center the specimen over the hole in the stage. Secure the slide with the stage clips.

FIGURE 15.
●●●●●●●●●●●●●●

Microscopic Examination of Trace Evidence

(a)

Student Microscope

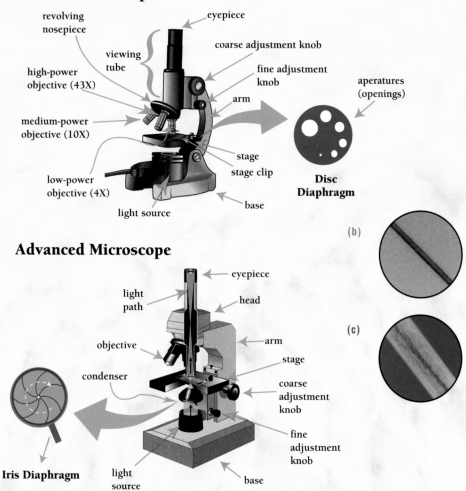

- revolving nosepiece
- eyepiece
- coarse adjustment knob
- viewing tube
- high-power objective (43X)
- fine adjustment knob
- aperatures (openings)
- medium-power objective (10X)
- arm
- low-power objective (4X)
- stage
- stage clip
- base
- light source

Disc Diaphragm

Advanced Microscope

- eyepiece
- light path
- head
- objective
- arm
- stage
- condenser
- coarse adjustment knob
- fine adjustment knob
- **Iris Diaphragm**
- light source
- base

(b)

(c)

(a) Compound microscopes.

(b) Human hair at 60X magnification.

(c) Human hair at 430X magnification.

●●●●●●●●●●●●●●●

5. Watching from the side, carefully lower the objective, moving it down toward the microscope slide by turning the coarse adjustment knob clockwise.

6. Look through the eyepiece and use the coarse adjustment knob to focus upward, away from the microscope stage and the microscope slide. Try to bring the fiber image into rough focus. If you go too far, begin again at Step 5.

7. Use the fine adjustment knob to bring the fiber image into sharp focus. Look into the eyepiece and observe the fiber. It will be small in size. Move the slide on the stage until the fiber is centered.

8. Controlling the amount of light that passes through the fiber—what microscopists call contrast—is important for proper viewing. Too much light washes out the image, making it hard to see details. The iris diaphragm—similar to the iris of your eye—controls the amount of light reaching the slide. Adjust the iris diaphragm for best lighting. You will need more light (a wider diaphragm opening) at higher magnifications. Best contrast occurs as the field of view just begins to darken as you observe it through the eyepiece. If you close the iris too much, the viewing area will appear dark and muddy. *Note:* Some compound microscopes have a disc diaphragm instead of an iris diaphragm—a series of small to large round openings on a wheel that can be moved to control the size of the light beam.

9. To switch to a higher magnification, carefully turn the revolving nosepiece and bring the next higher power objective (10X) into position over your fiber sample. (Now the total magnification will be 10X objective × 10X eyepiece = 100.) You will feel a click or a bump as the new objective locks into place. You should only have to use the fine adjustment knob, focusing upward, to achieve a sharp focus. Remember to never focus downward. Doing so could drive the objective into your slide and damage the slide and the objective!

10. View most fiber evidence at 400–430X magnification. To do this, switch to the highest power objective (40X or 43X). Now the total magnification will be 10 × 40 = 400, or 10 × 43 = 430. Be sure to adjust the iris or disc diaphragm for best contrast.

The compound microscope needs to be calibrated so that viewed objects can be measured. The width of the viewing area, or field diameter, at a total magnification of 40X (10X eyepiece with a 4X objective lens) is approximately 4 mm (4,000 µm) wide. That means the distance across the round field of view when you look through the microscope is 4 mm. If you can estimate how many widths of your fiber it will take to fill the area, you can estimate the size of your fiber (see Figure 16a). For example, it looks like you could line up about 20 of the hairs you see in Figure 16a to fill the

FIGURE 16.

Measuring with a Microscope

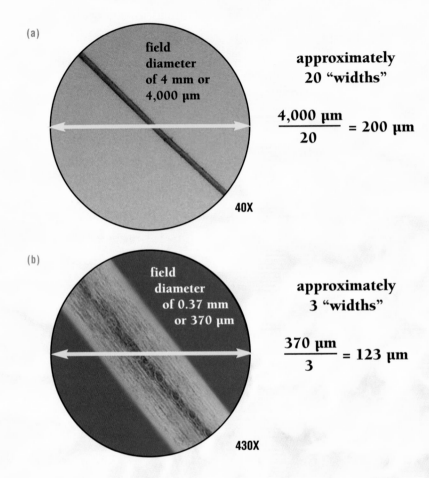

(a)

field
diameter
of 4 mm or
4,000 μm

approximately
20 "widths"

$$\frac{4,000 \ \mu m}{20} = 200 \ \mu m$$

40X

(b)

field
diameter
of 0.37 mm
or 370 μm

approximately
3 "widths"

$$\frac{370 \ \mu m}{3} = 123 \ \mu m$$

430X

(a) When you look under a microscope at 40X, you see this field of view. This round field of view is 4 mm (4,000 μm). The width of about 20 of these hairs will fit across the field, so $\frac{4,000 \ \mu m}{20}$ = 200 μm. The hair sample is about 200 μm wide.

(b) Under higher power, the field of view is only 370 μm. Since about three of the hair widths would fill the field, the size of the hair is $\frac{370 \ \mu m}{3}$ = 123 μm.

4-mm field of view. So the one hair fiber takes up about 1/20 of the viewing field. This makes the hair approximately 200 µm in diameter, because 4 mm ÷ 20 µm = 0.2 mm, or 200 µm.

Table 3 has the field diameters for most compound microscopes.

TABLE 3. Field Diameters for Varying Magnification

EYEPIECE MAGNIFICATION	OBJECTIVE MAGNIFICATION	TOTAL MAGNIFICATION	FIELD DIAMETER
10X	4X	40X	4 mm (4,000 µm)
10X	10X	100X	1.6 mm (1,600 µm)
10X	43X	430X	0.37 mm (370 µm)

Steps in Examining Unknown or Questioned (Q) Fibers

Use the following points as a guide, along with your reference collection, to help make your identification:

- Match fiber type to fiber type—animal, plant, synthetic.
- If hair—calculate and compare the medullary index and medullary type for hairs.
- If human hair—identify color, and any unusual characteristics.
- If plant fiber—what is the source?

- If synthetic—what is its color, physical appearance?
- Note any special features or unusual appearance.

Similarity and Dissimilarity

Both known (K) and questioned (Q) samples are examined under various magnifications and light conditions. Similar samples share common features; dissimilar samples do not. It is the analyst's responsibility to determine whether a questioned (Q) sample shares common features with a known (K) sample.

Sometimes a compared fiber sample does not share *every* common feature with a known example. For example, there may not be enough fibers to make a conclusive comparison. In these cases, the microanalyst would have to conclude that the comparison is not clear-cut—therefore, inconclusive.

CHAPTER 3

Inspector's Casebook

The cases in this chapter are actual cases involving the use of trace and contact evidence that helped convict individuals. You will read about the forensic techniques investigators used to solve these cases. Then you will use similar detection skills to solve cases of your own.

CASE #1

The Case of the Quiet Transfer

OBJECTIVE: Examining how every contact leaves a trace

THE SCOUNDREL: Theodore Robert Bundy (1947–1989)

THE CRIME: MURDER. In February 1978, Ted Bundy was a man on the run. He had escaped from a Colorado jail—and a murder trial—two months earlier. Already a convicted felon, he was one of the ten most-wanted fugitives by the FBI. He traveled from Colorado to Ann Arbor, Michigan, then headed south to Florida.

In February, Bundy traveled from Tallahassee to Lake City, Florida. There, he attacked and murdered Kimberly Leach. On February 15, he was stopped by a

Pensacola police officer for a routine traffic violation. The police officer ran the license plate of the orange VW van. The vehicle was listed as stolen. Bundy was taken into custody, and his hidden identity was discovered.

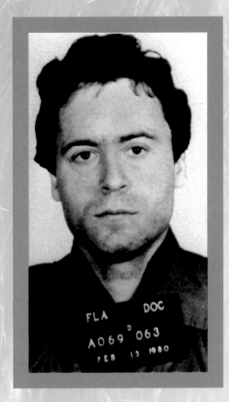

Ted Bundy in a 1980 police photo.

When the van was searched, bits of soil and leaves were found, along with other fibers and hairs. This trace evidence was analyzed and linked to the death and disappearance of Kimberly Leach.

Although Ted Bundy had already been convicted and sentenced to death for the killing of two Florida State University students, he also stood trial for the murder of Kimberly Leach. Forensic fiber evidence helped convict him. Lynn Hensen was a microanalyst assigned to the Leach case. She examined the fiber evidence and testified at the trial. Her analysis showed a mixture of a variety of fibers from a coat belonging to Bundy, carpeting in the stolen van, and clothing on the victim's body.

Hensen testified that it was "extremely probable" that the clothing of the defendant, the carpet in the van, and the victim's clothing had been in contact—each had exchanged trace evidence. During the trial, she told the jury that the exchange of material from one person to another can occur.

In late June 1981, the press interviewed Lynn Alan Thompson, Bundy's lawyer. He told the interviewer that Ms. Hensen's expert testimony was critical in persuading the jury to convict his client. On January 24, 1989, Ted Bundy was electrocuted by the State of Florida for the murder of Kimberly Leach.

PROJECT:

Every Contact Leaves a Trace

Edmond Locard (1877–1966) first proposed the idea of a material exchange principle—"It is impossible for a criminal to act, especially considering the intensity of a crime, without leaving traces of his presence."

Let's investigate to see if a contact leaves a trace.

What You Need:
- an adult
- access to a washer and dryer
- white T-shirt
- some friends

- notebook
- pen or pencil
- access to a carpet
- access to a pet
- single-color sweater
- paper bag(s)
- tweezers, fine point
- paper envelope(s)
- permanent black ink marker
- clear sticky tape (3/4-inch)
- microscope slides
- light corn syrup
- paper cup
- medicine dropper
- cover slips
- fiber reference collection (see page 36)
- newspaper
- magnifying glass (10–20X)
- compound microscope

What You Do:

1. Under adult supervision, wash a white T-shirt to remove any stray attached fibers.
2. Dry the T-shirt, outside, if possible, on a clothesline. Or, dry it, alone, in a clothes dryer.
3. Put the T-shirt on.
4. Have a friend keep very close track of your activities, paying careful attention to the order in which you do them. Make sure your friend records in the notebook exactly what you do next, and where you do it.

5. Do one or all of the following contact exercises: rolling on a carpet, roughhousing with another friend wearing a single-color sweater, and playing with the family dog or other pet.

6. After your activities, remove the T-shirt and place it in a paper "evidence" bag.

7. Use the collecting techniques (see Chapter 2) to collect known (K) fiber samples from each activity location. Label all collected samples.

8. Use tweezers to remove collected individual fibers from the collection envelope. Make a labeled, permanent mount (see Figure 14) of each collected known fiber type.

9. Record each sample in your notebook, e.g. "K-1," K-2," etc.

10. Spread out a newspaper. Carefully open the evidence bag containing the T-shirt and place it on the newspaper.

11. Use a magnifying glass to "scan" an area of the T-shirt. Use tweezers to pick up large fibers, or collect them using the lift tape method (see Figure 2). Label collected samples from the T-shirt— e.g. "Q-1," "Q-2," etc. Examine the entire shirt on both sides.

12. Examine the fiber evidence with a magnifying glass and/or under the microscope (see Figure 15).

See Chapter 5 for a sample analysis.

Tips For Analyzing Hair and Fiber Evidence

1. Begin with the collected fibers from each known (K) source.

2. Try to carefully and fully describe each known (K) fiber. Record these descriptions and drawings in your notebook. Figure 17 shows an analysis of a carpet sample.

3. After you have identified and described known (K) fibers from each location, do the same with the numbered (Q) samples collected from the T-shirt.

4. For each recovered Q fiber, see if you can get a match to a K fiber. For example, you recover a green fiber from the T-shirt. The carpet color is green. When both fibers are compared, they appear to have *similar* characteristics.

Science Project Idea

During his professional career, Edmond Locard handled many cases. One interesting case involved the matching of a red powder (ferric oxide or jeweler's rouge) found on the victim to a maker of eyeglass lenses.

Another unique powder is diatomaceous earth, a filter material used in pool filters. This white powder is made of tens of millions of tiny silica shells. Obtain some diatomaceous earth powder at a local pool supplier. Also obtain some talcum powder from a

FIGURE 17.

Analysis of a Carpet Sample

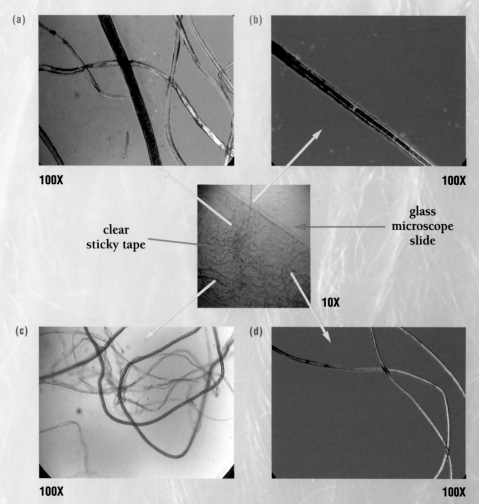

(a) 100X

(b) 100X

clear sticky tape

glass microscope slide

10X

(c) 100X

(d) 100X

Use the tape lift method to collect carpet fiber samples.

Four different areas of the slide with the carpet samples show:

(a) tan polyester, dog hair, and green wool   (b) dog hair

(c) red cotton and blue rayon   (d) green wool

grocery store. Make a labeled, permanent mount preparation (see Figure 14) of each powder. Sprinkle a small amount of one of the white powders onto a colored T-shirt. Have your friends examine this trace evidence to find out if the "suspect" had access to a pool pump house. Be sure to illustrate and document your findings in your notebook.

CASE #2

• • • • • • • • • • • • • • •

The Case of the Confirming Impression

OBJECTIVE: Analyzing footprint impressions

THE ATTACKERS: Christopher Slavin (1972–   ) and Ryan D. Wagner (1982–   )

THE CRIME: ASSAULT. Israel Perez Arvizu and Magdaleno Estrada Escamilla were looking for jobs. They needed to work to support their families back in Mexico. On the afternoon of September 17, 2000, two men drove up to Arvizu and Escamilla. These men promised the two immigrants work. Arvizu and Escamilla drove with the two men to a construction site in Suffolk County, New York.

Once inside an abandoned building, Arvizu and Escamilla were viciously attacked. Luckily, they managed to escape. They ran away from the abandoned building toward a nearby expressway. There they flagged down a passing motorist who contacted police.

Investigators began an intensive search of the area. They found blood drops near the building. A blood trail led away from the building toward the expressway. They also found blood evidence in the attackers' car, and on a posthole digger left inside the abandoned building. A Suffolk County police officer, John White, found a fresh footprint in the soft soil just outside the building. They photographed the footprint and made a cast of it.

Shortly after arriving on the scene, police picked up two men, Ryan Wagner and Christopher Slavin. They were identified as the attackers by the two victims. Both Wagner and Slavin denied any knowledge of the attack.

At the Suffolk County Crime Laboratory in Hauppauge, New York, forensic scientists were at work evaluating the evidence. Ann Juston, a forensic blood specialist, found that blood DNA found in the car driven by the assailants matched Ryan Wagner's DNA. She also found that blood on the posthole digger matched one of the victim's blood, and blood outside the building matched the other victim.

Another forensic scientist, Donald Doller, found that the outline of the shoe print found at the scene matched the size and shape of a boot belonging to one of the attackers. Later in court, Doller testified that this outline was "consistent with the sole of a black lace-up boot belonging to Christopher Slavin."

Slavin and Wagner were eventually convicted of assault in separate trials. Both were sentenced to twenty-five years in prison and were fined. At his trial, Wagner stated: "I have great remorse for what I did." But Judge Stephen L. Braslow told the young man: "You were sorry and remorseful after you got caught."

PROJECT:

Making Impression Casts

What You Need:

- sand or soil impression (footprint or tire mark)
- camera (optional)
- white card
- cardboard
- scissors
- stapler
- tablespoon
- plaster of Paris
- container for mixing plaster of Paris
- measuring cup
- water
- plastic bag
- soft artist's paintbrush
- ink pad (optional)
- rag (optional)
- graph paper (optional)

What You Do:

1. Select a distinct impression that you wish to cast, such as a footprint or tire mark in sand or soil. Photograph it, if possible, before casting. To improve the contrast in your photograph, use a white card to reflect light onto the impression from the side (see Figure 18).

2. To create a one-inch-high mold around the impression, cut some cardboard into one-inch strips and

FIGURE 18.

Making an Impression Cast

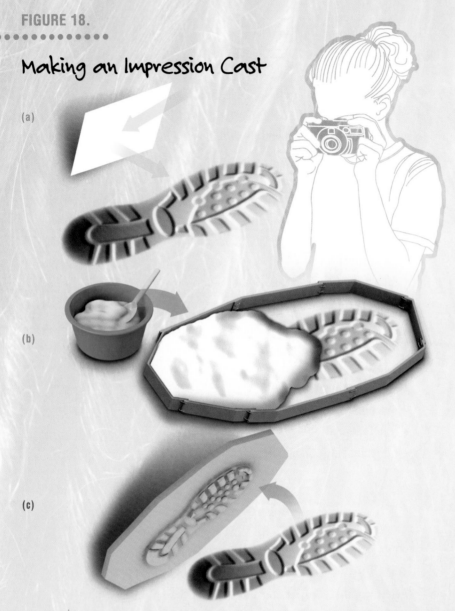

(a) Find a suitable impression and photograph it. Use a white card to reflect light onto the sides of the impression, providing contrast around these edges.

(b) Create a mold and fill it with plaster of Paris.

(c) Remove the mold and wipe it clean.

staple them together to form one long strip. Bend and staple the cardboard strip into a circle or oval large enough to surround the impression. Position the cardboard mold in the soil or sand, surrounding the impression. The mold will help you handle the cast.

3. Spoon 8 to 12 tablespoons of plaster of Paris into a container along with approximately two cups of water. Use a tablespoon to mix the plaster of Paris until it becomes thick. Stir it well—but slowly—to avoid creating bubbles in the plaster, which can produce holes in the cast. Depending on the size of the cast, you may need to make more plaster.

4. Carefully pour or spoon the mixed plaster into the mold. Fill the mold to at least cover half an inch depth. Allow the plaster to harden overnight. It is a good idea to cover the mold with a plastic bag so that rain will not affect the plaster cast.

5. The next day, tap the top of the mold with your finger to confirm that the plaster has hardened. Carefully lift the mold and use a soft artist's paintbrush to gently remove any dirt or sand from the bottom of the cast. You may choose to remove the cardboard from the cast as well.

If the pattern on the bottom of the cast is difficult to see, you can use ink to give it more contrast. Apply some ink with a rag that has been dipped on an inkpad. If you are making casts of a number of similar types of impressions (bicycle tire tracks for example), you may want to use an inked cast as a stamp to make a print on a piece of paper. This will create a record sheet. The recorded markings can then be measured and compared.

Can you match the stamped record of the track to a specific shoe or tire? What affects the quality of your cast? Do deeper prints make better casts? Does wetter soil or sand help create a better cast? Conduct more experiments to find out.

CASE #3

The Case of the Implicating Fabric

OBJECTIVE: Learning about fabric identification and comparison

THE TERRORISTS: Abdel Basset Ali al-Megrahi and Al Amin Khalifah Fhimah

CRIME: TERRORIST ATTACK. On December 21, 1988, Pan Am Flight 103 was blown up as it flew over Lockerbie, Scotland. Two pounds of plastic high explosive were remotely detonated in the cargo hold of the aircraft—259 people aboard died. Eleven people also died on the ground.

The Lockerbie bombing was investigated for over three years by three police agencies, including the Federal Bureau of Investigation (FBI). Over a thousand Scottish police officers and members of the British Army searched an area of more than 845 square miles. Their instructions were: "If it isn't growing and it isn't a rock, pick it up."

The aircraft was reconstructed in Farnborough, England. Investigators found evidence of an explosion on the left side of the aircraft in the area of the forward cargo hold.

The detailed police searches around Lockerbie turned up fifty-six fragments of a suitcase that showed evidence of significant blast impact damage, meaning that the suitcase may have contained the plastic explosive. Who did the suitcase belong to? With the help of luggage manufacturers, investigators determined that it was a brown Samsonite suitcase.

In Lockerbie, Scotland, the site of the Pan Am Flight 103 crash held evidence that linked the suspect's luggage to the bomb.

Examination of fragments of various cloth fabrics believed to have been in the Samsonite suitcase showed fragments of a Toshiba RT-SF 16 Bombeat radio cassette player embedded into them. The cloth fabrics were identified as:

- blue infant Babygro
- Primark jumpsuit
- white cotton Abanderado T-shirt
- cream-colored cotton pajamas
- knitted brown woolen cardigan with the label "Puccini Design"
- herringbone weave fabric that had a label indicating it came from a pair of size 34 Yorkie men's trousers

Contained within the trouser fabric were clumps of blue and white fibers consistent with the blue jumpsuit material. Investigators discovered that Yorkie trousers are manufactured in Ireland and Malta by Yorkie Clothing. (The Republic of Malta is a small island in southern Europe.) In August 1989, Scottish detectives flew to Malta to speak to the owner, Toni Gauci.

Gauci recalled that, about two weeks before the bombing, he had sold Yorkie trousers to a man who spoke English and Arabic with a distinctive Libyan accent. He remembered the sale, he told the police, because the customer did not seem to care what he was buying. He bought an old tweed jacket, a blue Babygro jumpsuit, a woolen cardigan, and a number of other clothing items, all of different sizes. Gauci described the man as 5 feet 10 inches tall, muscular, and clean shaven.

A Scottish police artist flew to Malta to make a detailed sketch of the man based on Gauci's description. This sketch led investigators to Abdel Basset Ali al-Megrahi—a Libyan intelligence officer and the head of security for Libyan Arab Airlines and a relative of Libyan President Mu'ammar Gadhafi.

Investigators also traced the origin of every piece of luggage that had been checked onto Pan Am Flight 103. After careful review, investigators learned that Megrahi had been a passenger on a Libyan Arab Airlines flight that arrived in Malta. They also discovered that he had a bag transferred from this flight onto other flights that later connected with Pan Am Flight 103. Megrahi was not on Pan Am Flight 103—but the unaccompanied bag was. But how could Megrahi's bag be transferred without arousing suspicion?

Authorities also learned that Megrahi's friend, Al Amin Khalifah Fhimah, was the station manager for Libyan Arab Airlines in Malta. The forensic connection between Fhimah, Megrahi, and the unaccompanied bag was made.

Murder indictments (formal accusations of a serious crime) were issued on November 13, 1991, against Abdel Basset Ali al-Megrahi and Al Amin Khalifah Fhimah.

The trial in the Netherlands opened on May 3, 2000—eleven years after the bombing. After months of forensic testimony, verdicts were reached on January 31, 2001. Megrahi was found guilty and sentenced to life in prison in a Glasgow prison. Fhimah was found not guilty. He returned to Libya the next day.

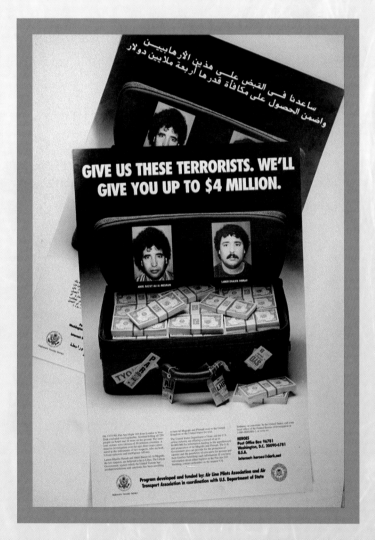

A wanted poster describes the reward for Abdel Basset Ali al-Megrahi and Al Amin Khalifah Fhimah, the terrorist suspects in the bombing of Pan Am Flight 103.

PROJECT:

Learning Weave Patterns

Fabrics or cloths are made by interweaving threads or yarns on a machine called a loom. These threads and yarns are either of natural or synthetic fiber. Some weave patterns, like a plain weave, produce smooth flat fabric. Other fabric weaves, like terry cloth, have a raised surface of projecting threads called a pile.

What You Need:

- fabric examples from a fabric store (terry cloth, handkerchief, felt, corduroy, denim, satin, calico, tweed, velvet)
- envelopes
- pencil
- magnifying glass (5–20X)
- some friends

What You Do:

1. Visit a fabric store. Ask the clerk for some small fabric samples.
2. Place each sample in an envelope labeled with its correct description.
3. Use a magnifying glass to carefully examine the surface of each fabric type. Compare your observations to the illustrations and photos in Table 4. Practice identifying each of the fabrics; can you correctly match the weave pattern?
4. Have your friends give you various unknown samples to identify. How "expert" are you at identifying weave patterns?

TABLE 4. Weave Patterns

WEAVE TYPE	WEAVE PATTERN	COMMON FABRICS	COMMON USES
PLAIN		• COTTON CALICOS • CHEESECLOTH • GINGHAM	• CURTAINS • HANDKERCHIEFS • TABLECLOTHS
TWILL		• DENIM • SERGE • TWEED	• PILLOWS • UPHOLSTERY • CLOTHING
SATIN		• SATIN	• DRAPERIES • CLOTHING
UNCUT PILE		• TERRY CLOTH	• TOWELS • ROBES • CARPET • AREA RUGS
CUT PILE		• CORDUROY • VELVET • VELVETEEN	• UPHOLSTERY
FELT		• FELT	• CRAFTS

CASE #4

●●●●●●●●●●●●●●●●●●●

The Case of the Incriminating Headlamp

OBJECTIVE: Identifying fragments

THE SCOUNDREL: Fracóis Latendresse

CRIME: HIT-AND-RUN HOMICIDE. In Rosemere, Quebec, Canada, a tragic hit-and-run accident occurred in 1995. A bicyclist was struck and killed. Provincial police recovered some glass fragments along with some red paint chips. Forensic scientists examined this trace evidence. The glass fragments were from the vehicle's headlamp. One of the glass fragments contained a code number. This number told investigators that the headlamp was from a Dodge Durango truck. Paint chip analysis told them that the truck was red. The search finally led Canadian authorities to Fracóis Latendresse. With the aid of New Jersey State Police, Latendresse was tracked and extradited (handed over to the jurisdiction of a foreign country) back to Canada. There he pleaded guilty to hit-and-run homicide.

PROJECT:

Identification Based on a Physical Property

Many common materials are difficult to describe. Although there are well over 100,000 kinds of glass, the vast majority (over 99 percent) that is encountered in forensic investigations is ordinary soda-lime glass. Glass fragments from broken windows and headlamps can be identified only through their physical properties. (The only way to conclusively match pieces of glass is to physically match their edges.) Physical properties of materials can provide valuable supportive information in a forensic investigation.

One physical property that is universally used is density—the relationship between an object's mass and its volume. For glass, forensic investigators have calculated that the odds of finding two random types of glass matching in density is well over 800:1.

What You Need:

- glass fragments (from auto collision shop)
- tweezers or forceps (to handle glass pieces)
- metric electronic balance (as sensitive as possible, measuring at least one decimal place)
- narrow graduated cylinder
- water

What You Do:

Determining an Object's Density

SAFETY: **Always use tweezers when handling glass fragments.**

1. Obtain half-inch-square (or larger) safety glass fragments from an automotive collision shop. Weigh a glass fragment on an electronic balance. The more sensitive your measurement, the more accurate your results. Measuring to two decimal places (0.01) is best.

2. To find the volume of the glass fragment, measure the amount of water it displaces. To do this, accurately record the volume of water in a narrow graduated cylinder. Drop the fragment into the water and record the new volume measurement. Subtract the beginning volume measurement from the ending measurement. The difference is the volume of the glass fragment. (If you cannot see a large enough increase in the volume of water, weigh more than one piece and place them all in the cylinder.)

3. Divide the mass of the sample(s) by the volume of water it (they) displaced. For example, if a glass fragment weighs 7.40 grams and displaces 3 mL of water, its density would be:

$$\text{Density} = \frac{\text{Mass}}{\text{Volume}} \quad \text{or} \quad \frac{7.40 \text{ g}}{3 \text{ mL}} = 2.47 \text{ g/mL}$$

Comparing Densities of Various Automotive Glass

There are three types of glass commonly used on automobiles: safety glass in the windshield, tempered glass in the side and rear windows, and common soda-lime glass in the headlamps. If possible, visit a couple of automotive glass sources (a junkyard or automotive window repair shop) and see if you can obtain pieces of each type of glass from each source. Take note of the visual appearance of any glass fragment. Safety glass breaks into square fragments, making its identification easy.

Find the densities of each of the glass pieces and compare them. For example, do glass windshield fragments from two different sources have identical densities?

Chapter 5 has analysis details.

Science Project Idea

Is all soda-lime glass the same? Suppose that as a forensic investigator, you are asked to determine if the soda-lime glass from a headlamp manufactured outside the United States differs from one produced domestically. Construct an outline for your study and proceed to collect data such as the names of the domestic and international headlamp manufacturers and the density of the glass for each headlamp. Visit junkyards and auto glass repair shops to obtain samples. Generally, foreign-produced automobile parts have specialized markings. **With adult permission**, use the Internet to help you learn more about these markings.

Write a science fair report; it should include your product search methods, density calculations, and close-up photographs.

CASE #5
●●●●●●●●●●●●●●●●

The Case of the Matching Hair Samples

OBJECTIVE: Using hair analysis to help make an identification

THE SCOUNDREL: Alex Mengel (1955–1985)

THE CRIME: MURDER. In the early evening of February 24, 1985, Westchester County police officer Gary Stymiloski pulled over a car. There were three people in the vehicle. The driver was thirty-year-old Alex Mengel. He and his two friends had been away in the Catskill Mountains for a day of target shooting.

While questioning Mengel, Stymiloski noticed used shotgun shells in the car. He returned to his police cruiser and called for assistance. For some strange reason, Mengel got out of his car and shot and killed Stymiloski. Mengel then fled the scene on foot.

On March 2, Mengel was spotted by two alert Canadian officers of the Ontario Provincial Police force (OPP). They ran the New York license plate of a vehicle driving suspiciously in Toronto, Canada. The family of the vehicle's registered driver, Beverly Capone of Mount Vernon, New York, had reported it missing on

February 26. She had last been seen on February 25, driving away from work.

The OPP officers attempted to stop the vehicle. Knowing that he was detected, Mengel tried to evade the officers. In the process, Mengel crashed the stolen car into a wall on a dead-end street. He was quickly captured and arrested. After searching the vehicle, officers found two pistols and a hair sample. Ballistics tests run by OPP forensics experts showed that one pistol had been recently fired. Later ballistics analysis would link it to the Stymiloski killing. Ontario police inspectors believed that Mengel was able to cross the border undetected by disguising himself as a woman.

OPP microanalysts compared the hair samples from a brush and comb taken from Beverly Capone's apartment. Through microscopic and DNA analysis they determined that there was a match to hair samples in the car. Ontario police officials notified the New York State Police of Mengel's capture and the recovery of Capone's vehicle.

The New York State Police had been searching for Beverly Capone. Based on Mengel's previous trip, they searched a cabin in the Catskills near Durham, New York. There they found clothing worn by Beverly Capone. Later, the woman's remains were discovered about a mile away from the cabin in heavy woods, under a pile of stones. Capone had been stabbed once in the chest.

On March 26, Canadian authorities ordered Mengel deported to the United States. He was then taken to Green County to appear in court for the murder of Beverly Capone. As he was being returned to the county jail, Mengel tried to escape from his state police escort. Even though he was chained and handcuffed, Mengel fought with the two guards who were transporting him. Mengel wrestled with one guard and took his gun. The driver shot and killed Mengel before Mengel was able to fire a shot.

PROJECT:

Analyzing Hair and Fiber Samples

At a fictional crime scene, the body of a young blond man—a local taxidermist—has been discovered in an alleyway of the small business district of Haines, Alaska. From the looks of things, there was quite a struggle. The Alaska State Police crime scene investigators have recovered hair fiber evidence at the scene. A number of eyewitnesses have identified an individual of Asian decent observed near the area where the body was found at about the time of the slaying. The authorities have detained a person of Asian decent.

Figure 19 shows photomicrographs of hairs found on the body that are not the victim's. You have been called in to conduct an expert analysis of this evidence and to advise the district attorney and police if there is enough physical evidence to consider this individual a suspect.

What You Need:

- **magnifying glass**
- **notebook**
- **ruler**
- **pen or pencil**

What You Do:

1. Carefully analyze the magnified images of each of the six fibers in Figure 19. Use Chapter 2 as a general guide. Use a magnifying glass if needed.

    In your notebook, record your analysis results for each fiber in the figure. Be sure your analysis covers these points:
    - Fiber type—confirm what type of fiber (animal, plant, synthetic) it is.
    - If hair—compare the medullary indexes and medullary type (see page 28).
    - If human hair—identify color and any unusual characteristics.
    - If plant fiber—what is the source?
    - If synthetic—what is its color and physical appearance?
    - Note any special features or unusual appearance.
2. Can any sample(s) be excluded?
3. Write a pre-trial report for the court.
    Chapter 5 has a sample analysis.

FIGURE 19.

Hair Evidence at the Crime Scene

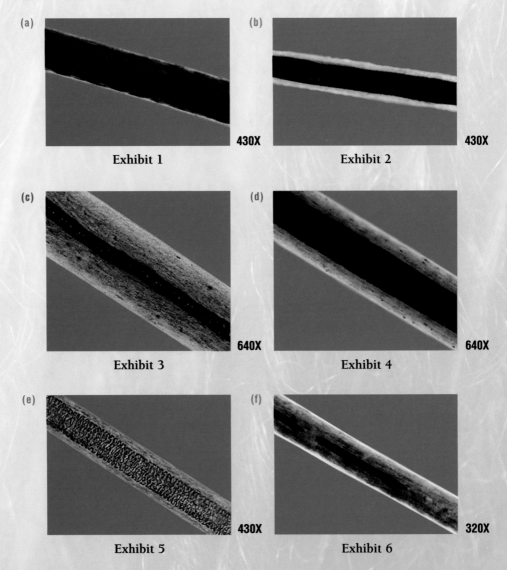

(a) 430X — Exhibit 1
(b) 430X — Exhibit 2
(c) 640X — Exhibit 3
(d) 640X — Exhibit 4
(e) 430X — Exhibit 5
(f) 320X — Exhibit 6

Fiber evidence collected at a crime scene. The hairs were found on the body, and do not belong to the victim.

CASE #6

●●●●●●●●●●●●●●●●●●

The Case of the Telling Red Paint Chip

OBJECTIVE: Identifying an unknown vehicle

THE SCOUNDREL: "Betty T." (1964–   )

CRIME: LEAVING THE SCENE OF A FATAL ACCIDENT. On the night of January 11, 1984, twenty-four-year-old Charles Accardi had just left a local bar. He began to walk home along the Jericho Turnpike in Syosset, New York. Earlier, twenty-year-old "Betty T." had gotten into her car—a red Toyota. She faced a long drive home to the quiet community of Woodbury, New York.

As close as police could estimate, Betty's car hit Accardi at approximately 1:30 A.M. on the Turnpike. Charles Accardi died instantly. Betty panicked, and drove home. She told her parents that her car was vandalized. The insurance company was contacted.

Accardi's body was discovered the next morning. Detectives recovered a chip of red paint from the dead man's raincoat. They also recovered pieces of a headlamp. The evidence was sent to the Nassau County crime lab.

At the lab, investigators turned to the P.D.Q. (Paint Data Query) computer program. The database has samples of 36,000 paint layers, nearly every type used on vehicles marketed in North America since the 1970s.

The Nassau investigators got an immediate match—the red paint chip came from a 1983 Toyota. An identifying mark on the headlamp piece was also a match to a Toyota. Case investigators immediately contacted Toyota dealers within the New York metropolitan area. They asked them to report any collision repair work on a red Toyota.

In late January, a Toyota technician in a Smithtown, New York, dealership was inspecting the front wheel well of a red Toyota. Jammed inside were fragments of what looked to be a raincoat. He contacted the Nassau police. The physical evidence match of the raincoat connected Betty T.'s vehicle to Charles Accardi.

In February 1986, Betty T. pleaded guilty to leaving the scene of a fatal accident. She was sentenced by a Nassau County judge to five years' probation and five hundred community service hours. Her driver's license was taken away.

PROJECT:

Analyzing Paint Chips

All paints have a solid portion called pigment. Pigment is responsible for the color of the paint. The liquid portion is called the vehicle, or solvent. Paints are applied in liquid form. As they dry, they become a thin, hard film. Paints harden by the evaporation of the solvent or by a chemical change called oxidation. Paints that harden by evaporation, like car paints, become so hard that they can break off in visible flakes. Paints that harden by the slower process of oxidation, such as oil paints on buildings, tend to peel off as an elongated ribbon or smear.

Frank S. Welsh is an expert in the microanalysis of paint. His company, Welsh Color & Conservation, Inc., has consulted with many historic building restorations, including the White House. In the next project, you will learn more about some of the microanalysis steps that experts take to reveal facts about a painted surface—how many layers of paint have been applied and their colors.

What You Need:

- an adult
- paint chip sample(s)
- tweezers
- magnifying glass (10–20X)
- notebook
- pen or pencil
- envelope or clear sandwich bag
- permanent black ink marker
- white index card, unlined
- single-edge razor blade
- modeling clay
- microscope slide
- black construction paper (2 x 3 inches)
- halogen desk lamp
- colored pencils

What You Do:

One quick method of examining a paint chip is to simply pick up a flake or ribbon with tweezers and examine its edge with a 10–20X magnifying glass. Be aware of which side is the inner and outer surface.

A more precise method follows here.

Obtaining Samples

1. Obtain permission from an adult to remove a small chip or ribbon of paint from a structure or other painted surface. Use tweezers to remove the sample. In your notebook, record which color is the outer surface. Place the chip or ribbon samples from a

single location in an envelope or clear sandwich bag. Label the envelope with the date, location, and color notations. Give each sample its own envelope and identification number.

Analyzing Samples

2. In your notebook, record the physical appearance of each numbered sample. Is it a flake (likely a non-oil-based paint) or a ribbon (an oil-based paint)?

3. Use tweezers to place the paint sample, outer surface facing you, in the center of a white index card. Use a single-edged razor to trim one side of the sample to create a straight edge.

4. Place a small piece of modeling clay in the center of a clean microscope slide.

5. Pick up the sample with tweezers and mount it in the clay so that its trimmed edge is at an upward angle.

6. Place the microscope slide on top of the trimmed 2 x 3-inch piece of black construction paper. Shine the light of a halogen desk lamp onto the mounted paint chip. Make sure that the upper surface of the paint chip is facing toward you.

7. Examine the mounted paint chip using a magnifying glass.

8. Carefully observe the various layers of paint or primer. Use colored pencils to draw what you see. How many distinct paint layers can you observe?

FIGURE 20.

Examining a Paint Chip

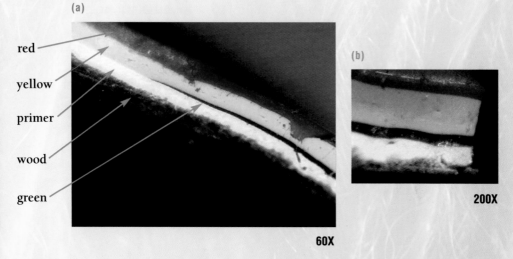

(a)

red

yellow

primer

wood

green

60X

(b)

200X

This magnified profile of a house paint chip shows different layers of paint that have been applied to the surface of the house.

How many colors have been applied? How thick are the layers? Figure 20 shows an example analysis of a paint chip.

Science Project Idea

What's in a paint job? With an adult, visit an automobile junkyard or a collision shop. With permission of the owner, take paint flake samples from various colored cars. Place individual paint samples in envelopes that are labeled with as much information as possible, including make of the vehicle, age, and paint color. Try to obtain paint samples from older vehicles (e.g., 1940s) and compare their paint to newer-model vehicles. Arrange your drawings of paint and underlying primer and undercoat colors by manufacturer and color. For example, did manufacturers of cars in the 1940s use overcoats? Primers?

Create an automotive paint chip reference collection. Have your friends present you with "unknowns" for you to identify.

The Case of the Missing Lynx

OBJECTIVE: Identifying animal hairs

ALLEGED CRIME: POSSIBLE BIOFRAUD. Recently, a new word—biofraud—has been created. Biofraud is the false reporting of data in a biological study. One case of alleged biofraud involved planting lynx fur during a government study.

The Canadian lynx (*Lynx canadensis*) is a 3 ½-foot-long wildcat that weighs up to 40 pounds. It has brownish-gray fur and black-tufted ears. It preys on the snowshoe hare (a kind of rabbit). The federal government is trying to protect lynx habitat in fifty-seven national forests in sixteen states.

The U.S. Forest Service and the U.S. Fish and Wildlife Service have been tracking the rare Canadian lynx to find out how many there are and where they live. Hair collection (fur sampling) is a new technique that wildlife biologists use to collect information about the habits of many animals without having to come in contact with the animals themselves. It is less stressful for the animal because it is not captured for sampling.

Today, the lynx and the grizzly bear are two animals sampled using this hair collection technique. It involves setting up hair trapping stations called "snags." In the lab, biologists use various microscopic and DNA techniques to identify collected hairs.

During the 1999 and 2000 sampling seasons, seven federal and Washington State biologists collaborated to send fraudulent fur samples to the lab for analysis. The hair samples were from a captive (not held in the wild) lynx and a bobcat (*Felis rufus*) pelt. With the submitted samples, the paperwork that the biologists included stated that they came from the Wenatchee and Gifford

Canadian lynx

Pinchot National Forests. The consequences of confirming lynx in these areas would be significant. The government would most likely take drastic steps to protect the wildcat's habitat.

Late in 2000, the study leaders were puzzled. The lab results did not seem to match. They seemed to have the same animal appearing in two different national forests that were far apart. They asked an independent scientist to review the data. The expert agreed—the data was just not believable. Additional DNA tests were done on the hairs. These tests showed that the hairs were linked to a bobcat, not a lynx.

If the original fur-sampling data had been acted on, the government would have likely banned many types of recreation and land use in both national forests in Washington State.

The seven biologists, who were not identified by the government, said their intent was only to test the lab's ability to identify lynx hair, not commit fraud. But several high-ranking members of Congress demanded an investigation. Their opinion was that these biologists were trying to influence a government action. In some circles, criminal charges were even discussed.

In March 2002, a report by Interior Department Inspector General Earl Devaney found no criminal intent on the part of the biologists involved. The Justice Department declined to prosecute them.

PROJECT:

Identifying Animal Hair

You are a microanalyst working in a forensic lab. You have been asked to help in an investigation. A conservation officer has reason to believe that deer in the area are being illegally hunted.

The investigation began in early October when a caller reported seeing blood and drag marks on a country road. This physical evidence suggested that an animal had been shot in the field, dragged, and loaded onto a roadside vehicle—probably a pickup truck.

Rifle season would not start in that particular area until the first of November. A conservation officer visited the scene. As a routine matter, the officer visited the home of the owner of the property. Parked in the drive was a white pickup truck. As the officer approached, he noticed blood and hair in the back of the truck. The property owner told the officer that he had been butchering cattle, and that he had a dog that always rode in the back of the truck.

The conservation officer asked if he could obtain hair samples. The owner agreed. Six evidence hair samples have been recovered and photographed (see Figure 21). They are ready for your analysis. Blood analysis confirmed the presence of cattle.

The director of the forensics lab wants the following questions answered:

FIGURE 21.

Identifying Animal Hair

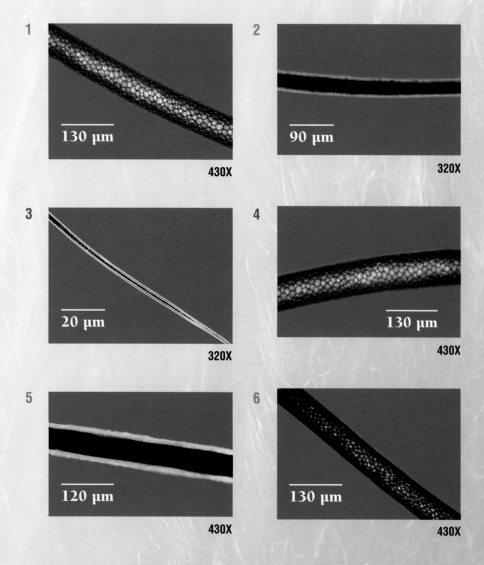

These collected fibers came from the bed of a pickup truck in Marion County, Montana.

- Was the property owner lying when he told the conservation officer that only cattle and the family dog were carried in the back of the pickup truck?
- Is there hair evidence of deer being transported in the pickup truck?

Be sure to include the following for each hair sample in your analysis:

  - Diameter of the hair shaft
  - Medullary index
  - Presence of ovoid bodies
  - Medulla type
  - Presence of pigment

- What are the sources of each hair?

Use Table 2 as a guide to your analysis. See Chapter 5 for analysis results.

Science Project Idea

See how good your friends are at spotting a fake. Ask them to make a microscopic identification of the alleged sable fur sample that you have provided. Visit a fabric store and ask for a sample of fake fur. Make permanent preparations (see Figure 14) of the fake fur and sable hair. Give the prepared slide of the fake fur to a friend and ask that your "microanalysis determination" be confirmed. Without looking at any reference slides, can your friend make the correct determination?

See Chapter 5 for analysis results.

•••••••••••••••••

The Case of the Recovered Cloth

OBJECTIVE: Investigating fabrics

THE SCOUNDREL: James P. Johnson (1950–   )

CRIME: VEHICULAR HOMICIDE. On the evening of Sunday, September 17, 2000, seventy-five-year-old Augusta Waddell was walking home on a dark road in Rostraver Township, Pennsylvania. Passing motorists noted that she wore a dark coat and walked unsteadily because she was using a cane.

When she did not return home, concerned family contacted the police. They searched along Fells Church Road. There they found the body of Waddell. At a nearby intersection, the thorough police investigation turned up two pieces of cloth. Police also found a paint chip and pieces of a car grille on the road. The investigators concluded that the hit-and-run had occurred at approximately 10:00 P.M.

Two weeks later, an anonymous tip led police to the driver, James P. Johnson. They examined his car, a 1987 Dodge Aries, and found several pieces of evidence that linked him to the hit-and-run incident. A piece of cloth was found in the wheel well of Johnson's car that appeared identical to that of Waddell's raincoat. It also matched the pieces of cloth found earlier along Fells Church Road. The hood had a chip in it. The recovered paint chip fit—exactly.

When questioned by police, Johnson claimed that he had hit a deer on Fells Church Road. He told police that he believed that he did not have to report the incident since it involved an animal.

At the garage where his car had been repaired, police recovered the car's damaged front grille. Back at the lab, they were able to match the recovered grille pieces from the road to the damaged grille at the garage. The lab technicians were also able to match the boot print from Waddell to the tread of a boot print found on the oil pan of the Dodge Aries. Trace evidence technicians had examined Johnson's vehicle closely. They found no hair evidence indicating that a deer had been struck.

At trial, Westmoreland County District Attorney John Peck argued that after Johnson hit Waddell he stopped the car at a nearby intersection and dislodged two pieces of her clothing still attached to the vehicle. On Friday, July 19, 2002, after deliberating just over two hours, the jury found Johnson guilty of involuntary manslaughter, vehicular homicide, and hit-and-run. He was sentenced to one-and-a-half to five years in prison.

PROJECT:

Examining Fabric Fibers: The Case of the Torn Sleeve

You will prepare special fiber evidence for your friends to examine.

What You Need:

- an adult
- handkerchief, new and unwashed
- sewing (shear) scissors
- tweezers
- clear ruler
- penknife
- manila envelope
- pen
- friends
- paper
- magnifying glass (10–20X)
- pencil
- notebook

What You Do:

Preparing the Evidence

Use Figure 22 as a guide.

1. Ask an adult for permission to cut a new, unwashed handkerchief.

FIGURE 22.

Preparing the Evidence

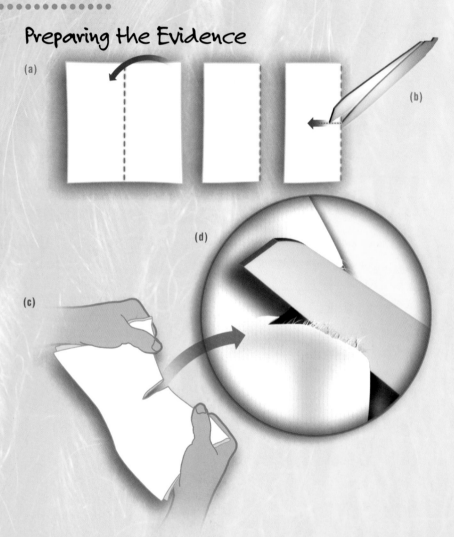

(a) Fold a new handkerchief in half.

(b) Use sewing shears to make a 1-inch cut perpendicular to the fold.

(c) Ask an adult to grasp both ends of the fold where the cut was made and tautly hold them apart in the shape of an "L."

(d) Rub the cutting edge of the shears along both cut edges, from the fold inward about ½ inch to fray the edges.

2. Fold the handkerchief in half. Use sewing shears to make a one-inch cut perpendicular to the fold, in the center.

3. **Ask an adult** to grab the cut edge and hold it in an "L" shape (see Figure 21c). Carefully rub the edge of the shears along the two edges of the cut cloth to roughen it up. Start at the folded end and rub inward about ½ inch.

4. Open up the cloth, shake it, and carefully fold it into thirds. Place the cloth into a manila envelope and seal.

5. Use a pen to mark the outside of the manila envelope with the following information:

   E V I D E N C E
   Portion of sleeve from work smock, property of
      Beatrix Rainis
   Submitted by worker for examination: 10–18–06
   State Workers' Comp Board

6. Provide this physical evidence to a friend who will examine it and prepare a report to the State Workers' Comp Board. Do NOT tell your friend what you have done in preparing the evidence. Include the following background information on a separate sheet of paper concerning the evidence:

   The cloth is a portion of the sleeve of a worker, Ms. Beatrix Rainis, who claims that it was caught in a machine. In so doing, Ms. Rainis claimed that the caught sleeve dragged her arm into the working parts of the machine and injured her hand.

There are no visible signs of injury, and X-rays show no internal bone damage. Ms. Rainis states that she is entitled to worker's compensation benefits. She has petitioned the Workers' Compensation Board for five months of back wages due to her injury. The sleeve is provided as evidence of machine damage.

Analysis

As a consultant microanalyst, you have been asked to read the background information and review the evidence provided to you. The Workers' Comp Board would like a detailed analysis that answers the central question: Does this fabric bear marks of tearing or cutting?

1. Remove the evidence from the sealed container.
2. Use a magnifying glass to carefully examine the entire length of the torn fabric.
3. Do you observe evidence of a tearing force on the fabric fibers? Or, do you observe that the fabric was cut? Use Figure 23 as a guide in determining which type of treatment was applied to the fabric—cutting or tearing.
4. You will need to write a report to the Workers' Comp Board. In the report, include:
   - your method of examination
   - photos or drawings of your findings
   - your conclusions
   See Chapter 5 for analysis results.

FIGURE 23.

Fabric Cuts vs. Tears

(a)

10X   60X

(b)

 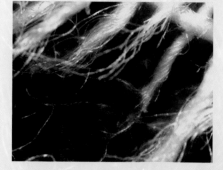

10X   60X

(a) Fabric cut
(b) Fabric tear

Investigating the Crime

This chapter introduces a "crime" that you and your friends can solve using the information and skills you learned in Chapters 2 and 3. The crime is based on an actual case. It is your responsibility to evaluate the presented evidence, reach conclusions, and provide findings of fact in a report to the director of the forensics laboratory.

THE PROFILE:

The Case of the Discarded Ghost

Judd Treadwell was found dead in the upstairs study of his Boston home. Earlier that evening, he had told guests at his Halloween party that he needed to excuse himself to conduct some needed business. He had been dressed in a yellow cotton sweater. His wife later found his body lying on the green wool carpet near his desk. There were signs of a struggle, and foul play is suspected—the police are treating the case as a homicide. The results of an autopsy are not yet complete.

Investigators have questioned, and accounted for, all the guests that attended the small early evening costume party—except for one, an individual who came as a ghost.

Several interviewed guests confirmed to police that the ghost danced at the party. One guest told investigators that he saw the ghost dancing with a woman—a brunette. She was wearing a large, fuzzy blue costume. Police interviewed the woman. She confirmed dancing with the ghost but said she did not know his identity. Investigators took samples of her hair and costume.

Several guests gave police the identity of the man in the ghost costume. When questioned at his home by police, Jerry Christianson denied being at the party. The police inspector wrote the following description of Christianson, a rather intense executive, in his notebook.

Name:	Jerry Christianson
Age:	34
Hair Color:	Blond, bleached
Stature:	Tall, about 6 feet, 2 inches; approximately 170 pounds
Notes:	States that he has a severe allergy to animal hair. Denies being at the costume party.

The forensics team found a discarded ghost costume behind a chair in the living room. Police recovered the white cotton fabric as evidence. They transported the evidence back to the lab. Investigator notes about the crime scene have also been included

Kitchen	tile floor
Living Room	blue carpet; ghost costume found behind a chair
Dining Room	tan carpet
Study (murder scene)	green carpet; throw rugs on furniture with heavy amounts of dog hair
Master Bedroom	red carpet
Basement	cat litter box

Additional field samples have also been transported to the lab:

- Paper envelope containing known green carpet fibers from the study
- Paper envelope containing known hairs from Jerry Christianson
- Paper envelope containing samples of dog hair from throw rugs in study
- Paper envelope containing samples of cat hair from throw rugs in study
- Paper envelope containing brown hair samples from a female guest
- Paper envelope containing blue costume "fur" samples from female guest
- Paper bag containing a yellow cotton sweater from Judd Treadwell

●●●

What You Need:

- an adult
- access to a dog and cat
- pet-grooming brush
- permanent marker
- paper envelopes
- strands of female human hair, natural brown
- strands of male human hair, blond
- strands of human hair, gray
- strands of human hair, black
- tweezers, fine point
- green carpet fibers (from your home, carpet store, or home supply store)
- yellow cotton fibers (from your home or fabric store)
- blue synthetic fibers (from your home or fabric store)
- cuticle scissors
- clear ruler
- white handkerchief, laundered, ironed, and folded in half
- paper grocery bag
- clear sticky tape (3/4-inch)
- friends
- compound microscope (400–430X magnification)
- microscope slides and coverslips
- light corn syrup
- roll of brown wrapping paper
- colored pencils
- notebook
- magnifying glass (10–20X)
- hair and fiber reference collection (Chapter 2)
- paper cup
- medicine dropper

What You Do:

Preparing the Evidence

1. COLLECT ANIMAL FIBERS: Ask an adult for permission for you to brush a pet cat and dog. You need not collect a great amount of animal hair. Brush the animals and collect hair samples. Place each hair sample type in a labeled envelope marked "EVIDENCE—dog hair Case No. 2006-1245" and "EVIDENCE—cat hair Case No. 2006-1245."

2. COLLECT HUMAN HAIR FIBERS: Ask permission to collect a few strands of hair from several individuals: Collect a few strands of natural brown hair from a female. If possible, include the root. Place entire strands in a labeled envelope marked "EVIDENCE—female hair sample Case No. 2006-1245."

   Collect strands of natural blond hair from a male. If possible, include the root. Place these hair strands in a labeled envelope marked "EVIDENCE—Suspect hair sample—Jerry Christianson Case No. 2006-1245."

   Collect black and gray hair samples. If possible, include the root. Place them inside an envelope marked "Hair samples."

3. COLLECT CARPET FIBERS: Use tweezers to pull fibers from a green carpet sample. Place the fibers in a labeled envelope marked "EVIDENCE—study carpet fibers Case No. 2006-1245."

4. COLLECT SWEATER FIBERS. With adult permission, use tweezers to pull yellow cotton fibers from a wool sweater, scarf, or wool hiking socks. Place the fibers in an envelope marked "EVIDENCE—sweater fibers Case No. 2006-1245."

5. COLLECT BLUE COSTUME FIBERS: Use tweezers to collect a few strands of synthetic blue fur. Use cuticle scissors to cut each strand into approximately 3-inch long pieces. Place these pieces in a labeled envelope marked "EVIDENCE—costume fur Case No. 2006-1245."

6. A white handkerchief will be a substitute for the entire white fabric ghost costume. It should be washed to remove all excess fibers.

7. Place the white handkerchief in a paper grocery bag. Keep the bag open.

8. Using tweezers, carefully open the following sample envelopes. Then place the designated number of fibers in a paper grocery bag.

   • CAT HAIR: place about 10 cat hair fibers inside the bag.

   • DOG HAIR: place about 10 dog hair fibers inside the bag.

   • STUDY CARPET: place 5 green carpet fibers inside the bag.

   • FEMALE HAIR: place 2 strands of natural brown hair inside the bag.

   • BLOND HAIR: place 2 strands of blond hair inside the bag.

- HAIR SAMPLES: place 2 black and 2 gray strands of hair inside the bag.
- SWEATER FIBERS: place 10 yellow cotton fibers inside the bag.
- BLUE FUR FIBERS: place 5 fake blue fur fibers inside the bag.

9. Use tweezers to place the clean handkerchief into the paper bag. Fold the top of the paper bag over on itself. Seal the bag using sticky tape.

10. Label the outside of the paper bag with a permanent marker:

> EVIDENCE
> 10-31-06
> Homicide
> Case No. 2006-1245
> White "Ghost" Costume
> Removed from: Treadwell Residence

Examining the Evidence

1. Provide all evidence and associated study materials to a friend whom you have asked to conduct the fiber analysis in this case.

Give the following to your friend:

- access to a compound microscope having 400–430X magnification
- needed materials to make prepared microscope slides:
  - glass microscope slides

- glass coverslips
- light corn syrup
- tweezers
- cuticle scissors
- permanent marker
- brown wrapping paper (or paper grocery bag)
- the nine labeled envelopes containing recovered KNOWN fiber samples
- EVIDENCE bag containing the ghost costume fabric.
- colored pencils
- notebook

2. Have your friend use cuticle scissors to cut a 2 x 3-foot piece of brown wrapping paper from its roll. Use tape to fasten it to the table where the examination will be made. Place the paper bag containing the suspect evidence in the center of the brown paper on the table. Use cuticle scissors to break the seal on the EVIDENCE bag containing the ghost costume. Carefully open the bag. Use tweezers to remove the "costume" (handkerchief) and place it on the brown wrapping paper.

3. Have your friend use a magnifying glass to carefully examine the surface of BOTH sides of the fabric, looking for evidence. Use Chapter 2 as a guide to collecting fiber evidence. As fibers are found, they should be collected using tweezers, and a permanent slide preparation immediately made (see Figure 14).

For long fiber evidence, your friend will need to cut the fiber into about 2½-inch lengths, each mounted on a separate microscope slide. Begin with the portion that has the root. If you do not have long, rectangular coverslips, position two square coverslips together to cover the fiber on the microscope slide. As each slide is made, use a permanent marker to label it. For example, a long fiber that needed three slides to mount would be labeled: "1a-2006-1245," through "1d-2006-1245."

4. Have your friend go over the fabric evidence at least twice so that he or she is confident that no fiber has been missed. Move the fabric to one side on the paper. Carefully shake the bag over the wrapping paper to check for any fallen fibers. If there are none, replace the fabric in the paper bag and reseal it.

5. Record each evidence number in a notebook, leaving space between numbers.

6. Use the microscope to examine each questioned (Q) fiber (see Figure 15). Examine the fibers at 400–430X magnification. You may want to use the hair and fiber reference collection from Chapter 2 to help you identify each fiber type—animal, plant, or synthetic. Use colored pencils to draw what you see on each slide. Do the drawings in your notebook. If the fiber is hair, calculate the medullary index and determine the medullary type. If it is human hair, identify color, and any unusual characteristics. If it

is a plant fiber, what is its source? If the fiber is synthetic, what is its color and physical appearance?

7. Examine known (K) fibers that were collected at the scene. Make a permanent prepared slide preparation from each marked evidence envelope. Label each of the slides with the known fiber identity— e.g. "cat hair." As in Step 6, examine these slides under the microscope at 430X. For each fiber record the following in your notebook: fiber type, thickness, characteristics, medullary index and type (if hair), color and appearance (if synthetic). Does examination under polarized light produce similar colors as a Q fiber of similar type?

   You should have examined each of the following known (K) fibers:

   • cat hair
   • dog hair
   • green carpet fibers from the study
   • yellow sweater fibers from the deceased
   • brunette hair from female guest
   • blond hair from suspect
   • blue fake fur
   • black and gray hair

8. Copy Table 5 into your notebook. Complete the table with your microscopic observations and calculations. Compare a (Q) fiber to its corresponding (K) fiber.

TABLE 5. Fiber Evidence Comparison

Q EVIDENCE NUMBER	COMMENTS	K KNOWN FIBER AND SOURCE	COMMENTS
	Fiber Type: Fiber Diameter: Medullary Index: Medulla Type: Scale Type: Color: Unusual Characteristics:		Fiber Type: Fiber Diameter: Medullary Index: Medulla Type: Scale Type: Color: Unusual Characteristics:

Analyzing the Evidence

Use your detailed colored drawings and your notes to record comparisons of the known and questioned fibers. See Figure 24 for an example of a photographic comparison of fibers, made by the author.

Complete Your Report

Your findings are important to the successful prosecution of the case. The lab director requests that the report contain the following:
- method(s) used in analysis
- findings:
- Were any fibers recovered from the white cloth costume?

FIGURE 24.
• • • • • • • • • • • • •

Fiber comparison—similarity vs. dissimilarity

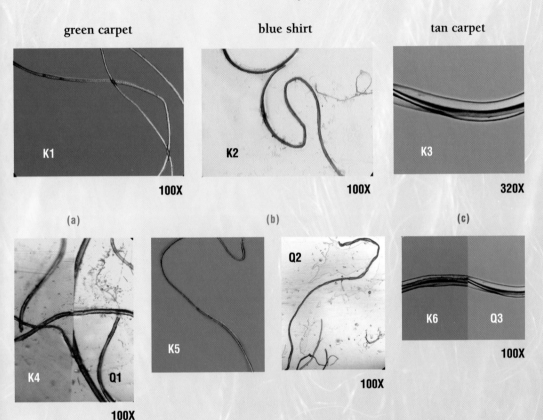

green carpet   blue shirt   tan carpet

The lab has recovered known (K) samples: green wool floor carpet fibers (K1), blue polyester dress shirt fibers (K2), and synthetic fibers from a tan floor carpet (K3). Three questioned (Q) fibers have been recovered from the white handkerchief: (Q1), (Q2), and (Q3). A comparison microscope analysis shows that

(a) The hunter green wool fibers (K4 / Q1) share similar characteristics.

(b) The blue fibers (K5) do not match a recovered blue cotton fiber (Q2).

(c) The known tan carpet fiber (K6) shares similar characteristics to a recovered fiber (Q3) from the white handkerchief.

ANALYSIS CONCLUSION: Fiber evidence does not connect the victim to the suspect.

• • • • • • • • • • • • • • •

- If so, list the recovered fibers.
- Are the recovered fibers similar to know fibers recovered at the scene?
- Can the fiber evidence be used to place the suspect at various rooms in the house, or near the victim?

Compare your findings to those in Chapter 5.

CHAPTER 5

Case Analyses

This chapter contains analysis findings for some of the cases presented in this book.

● ● ● ● ● ● ● ● ● ● ● ● ●

CASE #1. The Case of the Quiet Transfer

PROJECT: Every Contact Leaves a Trace

When the author did this project, he recovered tan fibers, dog hairs, and other animal hairs. Figure 25 shows an example comparison between his recovered fibers.

FIGURE 25. Analysis—Demonstrating Contact Transfer of Fibers

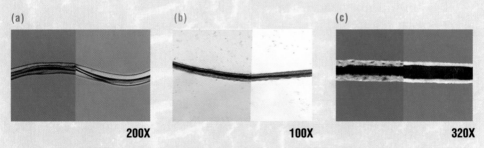

(a)   (b)   (c)

200X   100X   320X

(a) SIMILAR tan synthetic carpet fibers.

(b) SIMILAR hair fibers from the author's Tennessee Walker foxhound, Maggie.

(c) DISSIMILAR hair fibers: cow (L), horse (R).

• • • • • • • • • • • • • •

CASE #4. The Case of the Incriminating Headlamp

PROJECT: Identification Based on a Physical Property

Your density calculations should range between 2.47 and 2.56 g/mL for window glass; for headlamp glass the range would be 2.57 to 2.64 g/mL. The density of safety (windshield) glass is 2.3 g/mL.

• • • • • • • • • • • • • •

CASE #5. The Case of the Matching Hair Samples

PROJECT: Analyzing Hair and Fiber Samples

No synthetic or plant fibers were recovered. Four out of the six recovered hairs are animal (horse, beaver, dog, and muskrat). Two human hairs were recovered: black and brown. The recovered human black hair has a continuous medullary core. This fact, alone, is not enough to suggest that the detained individual was connected with the assault. You should suggest to the district attorney that this individual's coat be carefully examined for fiber evidence. Since the victim was a taxidermist, the recovery of unusual animal fibers from the scene that are consistent with the recovered evidence, and/or blond hairs, would add great weight to placing that individual at the scene. See Figure 26.

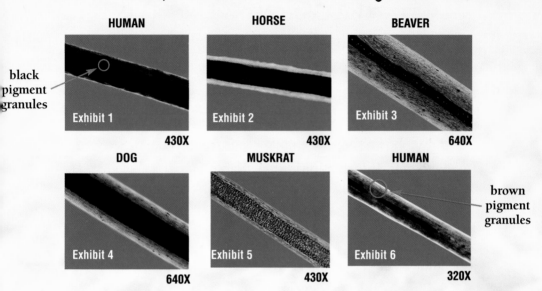

FIGURE 26. *Analysis—Case of the Matching Hair Samples*

THE CASE OF THE MATCHING HAIR SAMPLES: EVIDENCE INFORMATION TABLE					
EXHIBIT	FIBER TYPE	FIBER WIDTH (μm)	MEDULLA WIDTH (μm)	MEDULLARY INDEX	MEDULLARY TYPE; NOTES
#1	HUMAN; black	80	25	0.31	continuous medullary core; black/brown pigment
#2	ANIMAL; horse	120	85	0.71	amorphous medulla; cortical fusi
#3	ANIMAL; beaver	135	28	0.21	narrow lattice; medullary index below 0.50
#4	ANIMAL; dog	85	45	0.53	amorphous medulla
#5	ANIMAL; muskrat	115	70	0.61	aeroform lattice
#6	HUMAN; brown	80	20	0.25	interrupted medullary core; black/brown pigment

• • • • • • • • • • • • • • •

CASE #7. The Case of the Missing Lynx
PROJECT: Identifying Animal Hair

All exhibits are natural fibers. Exhibits #1 and #4 are deer hair. Exhibit #2 is cattle hair—consistent with blood analysis results. Exhibit #3 is cat hair and exhibit #5 is horse hair. Exhibit #6 is rabbit hair. See the Evidence Information Table (Table 6). Trace evidence confirms the presence of a deer carcass in the bed of the suspect's truck. However, there is no evidence to support when the deer hairs were deposited. The landowner cannot be issued a summons based solely on the fiber evidence developed in this case.

TABLE 6. The Case of the Missing Lynx: Evidence Information Table

Exhibit Number	Fiber Type/ Source	Diameter of Hair Shaft	Medulla Type	Medullary Index	Notes
#1	ANIMAL/ deer	78 μm	Wide lattice	0.88	Medulla covers almost entire hair shaft.
#2	ANIMAL/ cattle	54 μm	Amorphous	0.63	Many ovoid bodies. Brown pigment evenly distributed throughout cortex.
#3	ANIMAL/ cat	20 μm	Uniserial ladder	0.62	Medulla sharply tapers at end of hairshaft.
#4	ANIMAL/ deer	87 μm	Wide lattice	0.60	Medulla covers almost entire hair shaft.
#5	ANIMAL/ horse	76 μm	Amorphous	0.65	No ovoid bodies.
#6	ANIMAL/ deer	72 μm	Wide lattice	0.58	Medulla covers almost entire hair shaft.

Science Project Idea: Fake Fur

The questioned fiber (Q) is synthetic, not natural.

Exhibit Label	Fiber Type/ Source	Diameter of Hair shaft	Medulla Type	Medulla Width	Medullary Index
Q	Synthetic	112 µm	None	—	0
K	Natural: sable	126 µm	Wide lattice	77 µm	0.63

FIGURE 27. Analysis—Fake Fur

Exhibit 1–a

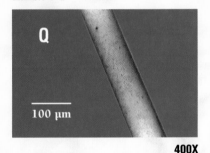

Exhibit 2–a

CASE #8. The Case of the Recovered Cloth

PROJECT: Examining Fabric Fibers: The Case of the Torn Sleeve

Ms. Rainis has committed a fraud. If events had happened as she had described, the entire length of the fabric tear would contain pulled, ragged threads. Individual thread fibers would be pulled and plainly visible. Other markings such as oil and grease stains should be evident if the fabric had gone through a machine. Also, one would expect numerous small tears, folds, and holes to also have been made in the sleeve fabric. Instead there is a single cut along the fabric, with a portion showing very consistent ragged edges. Such a result can be duplicated by first cutting the cloth, then taking a sharp blade (e.g. knife or scissors) and rubbing the edge to fray it. However, this action causes disruption of only that portion of the threads at the cut edge.

• • • • • • • • • • • • • • • • • • • •

CHAPTER 4

The Case of the Discarded Ghost

FINDINGS:

1. The following fiber types were recovered from the white cotton ghost costume:
   - cat hair fibers consistent with those taken from a throw in the basement
   - dog hair fibers consistent with those taken from a throw on a sofa in the study
   - a brown hair that is consistent with known (K) hairs taken from the female guest
   - a blue synthetic fiber that is consistent with a blue fiber taken from a costume from the female guest
   - bleached hair that is consistent with known (K) hairs taken from the suspect, Jerry Christianson
   - green wool carpet fiber that is consistent with known (K) fibers taken from the victim's study

- yellow wool fiber that is consistent with known (K) fibers taken from the victim's sweater

    Table 7 summarizes the comparison fiber data.

2. Based on the fiber evidence, the suspect, Jerry Christianson, can be forensically linked to the ghost costume. The ghost costume can be forensically linked to Treadwell's study.

    Figure 28 and Table 7 show an example analysis.

FIGURE 28. *Analysis—Case of the Discarded Ghost*

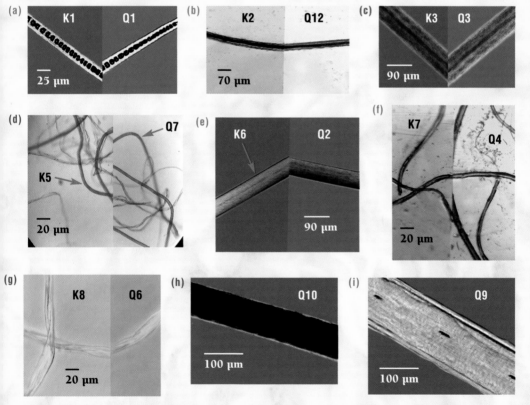

Microscopic comparison of known (K) versus questioned (Q) fibers recovered from the crime scene. (a) K1 vs Q1; (b) K2 vs Q12; (c) K3 vs Q3; (d) K5 vs Q7; (e) K6 vs Q2; (f) K7 vs Q4; (g) K8 vs Q6; (h) Q10; (i) Q9.

TABLE 7. Fiber Evidence Comparison

Q Exhibit Number (recovered from white ghost costume)	Comments	K (Known Fiber and Source)	Comments
1	Fiber Type: **cat hair** Fiber Diameter: **19 μm** Medulla Width: **10 μm** Medullary Index: **0.52** Medulla Type: **uniserial-ladder** Scale Type: **spinous** Color: **white** Unusual Characteristics: **no ovoid bodies**	**1** **cat hair— basement**	Fiber Type: **cat hair** Fiber Diameter: **19 μm** Medulla Width: **0.11 μm** Medullary Index: **0.57** Medulla Type: **uniserial-ladder** Scale Type: **spinous** Color: **white** Unusual Characteristics: **no ovoid bodies**
12	Fiber Type: **dog hair** Fiber Diameter: **72 μm** Medulla Width: **40 μm** Medullary Index: **0.56** Medulla Type: **amorphous** Scale Type: **imbricate** Color: **white** Unusual Characteristics: **no ovoid bodies**	**2** **dog hair— sofa in the study**	Fiber Type: **dog hair** Fiber Diameter: **70 μm** Medulla Width: **40 μm** Medullary Index: **0.57** Medulla Type: **amorphous** Scale Type: **imbricate** Color: **white** Unusual Characteristics: **no ovoid bodies**
3	Fiber Type: **human hair** Fiber Diameter: **90 μm** Medulla Width: **22 μm** Medullary Index: **0.24** Medulla Type: **continuous** Scale Type: **imbricate** Color: **brown** Unusual Characteristics: **brown pigment granules**	**3** **female guest**	Fiber Type: **human hair** Fiber Diameter: **92 μm** Medulla Width: **20 μm** Medullary Index: **0.22** Medulla Type: **continuous** Scale Type: **imbricate** Color: **brown** Unusual Characteristics: **brown pigment granules**
7	Fiber Type: **synthetic** Fiber Diameter: **40 μm** Medulla Width: **n/a** Medullary Index: **n/a** Medulla Type: **n/a** Scale Type: **n/a** Color: **blue** Unusual Characteristics: **solid fiber; no holes**	**5** **costume of a female guest**	Fiber Type: **synthetic** Fiber Diameter: **40 μm** Medulla Width: **n/a** Medullary Index: **n/a** Medulla Type: **n/a** Scale Type: **n/a** Color: **blue** Unusual Characteristics: **solid fiber; no holes**
2	Fiber Type: **human hair** Fiber Diameter: **90 μm** Medulla Width: **not observed** Medullary Index: **n/a** Medulla Type: **n/a** Scale Type: **imbricate** Color: **bleached** Unusual Characteristics: **"highlighted"; faint medullary core observed**	**6** **Jerry Christianson**	Fiber Type: **human hair** Fiber Diameter: **90 μm** Medulla Width: **25 μm** Medullary Index: **0.27** Medulla Type: **interrupted medullary core** Scale Type: **imbricate** Color: **bleached** Unusual Characteristics: **"highlighted"**

TABLE 7. Fiber Evidence Comparison (continued)

Q Exhibit Number (recovered from white ghost costume)	Comments	K (Known Fiber and Source)	Comments
4	Fiber Type: **wool (sheep)** Fiber Diameter: **21 µm** Medulla Width: **n/a** Medullary Index: **n/a** Medulla Type: **n/a** Scale Type: **imbricate** Color: **green** Unusual Characteristics: **dyed**	**7** **victim's study**	Fiber Type: **wool (sheep)** Fiber Diameter: **20 µm** Medulla Width: **n/a** Medullary Index: **n/a** Medulla Type: **n/a** Scale Type: **imbricate** Color: **green** Unusual Characteristics: **dyed**
6	Fiber Type: **cotton** Fiber Diameter: **25 m** Medulla Width: **n/a** Medullary Index: **n/a** Medulla Type: **n/a** Scale Type: **n/a** Color: **yellow** Unusual Characteristics: **twisted; dyed**	**8** **victim's study**	Fiber Type: **cotton** Fiber Diameter: **20 µm** Medulla Width: **n/a** Medullary Index: **n/a** Medulla Type: **n/a** Scale Type: **n/a** Color: **yellow** Unusual Characteristics: **treated cotton (fewer twists than untreated)**
10	Fiber Type: **human hair** Fiber Diameter: **100 µm** Medulla Width: **14 µm** Medullary Index: **.14** Medulla Type: **continuous** Scale Type: **imbricate** Color: **black** Unusual Characteristics: **high concentration of black pigment**		
9	Fiber Type: **human hair** Fiber Diameter: **100 µm** Medulla Width: **12 µm** Medullary Index: **0.12** Medulla Type: **interrupted medullary core** Scale Type: **imbricate** Color: **gray** Unusual Characteristics: **loss of pigment**		

GLOSSARY

bleaching—Chemical or a natural process used to make a hair colorless or lighter than its usual color.

Caucasian—A term designating one of the major groups of human beings originating from Europe.

comparison microscope—A type of microscope that allows two views to be compared together or combined.

compound microscope—A type of microscope that uses two lenses (or combination of lenses), an objective lens and an eyepiece lens, to focus a greatly magnified image of the subject on the retina of the observer's eye.

consistent—To be similar to.

continuous medulla—A medulla of a hair sample that has no disruptions.

cortex—The region of a hair between the cuticle and the medulla. It is composed of elongated and spindle-shaped cells.

cortical fusi—Small spaces that appear in the hair shaft.

cuticle—The outermost region of a hair composed of layers of overlapping scales.

dissimilar—Not similar.

dye—A chemical used to artificially color something, such as hair.

evidence—Testimony, documents, or material objects presented at a trial to prove the existence or nonexistence of a fact.

fiber—A thread from animal or plant tissue.

findings—Legal conclusions acceptable by a court.

fraud—An action with intent to deceive.

hair—Fibrous outgrowth from the skin of mammals.

hair identification—Process of classifying a given hair as a member of a defined class of hairs (e.g., human, animal).

GLOSSARY

●●●

imbricate—Hair scale pattern with edges overlapping in a wavy pattern. This pattern is typical of human hair.

impression evidence—Evidence—such as tire tracks, footprints, fingerprints, tool marks, and bite marks—at a crime scene.

magnification—The amount the size of an object is increased when viewed.

medulla—The core of the hair shaft.

melanin—A natural pigment that determines the color of human and animal hair.

microanalyst—A person trained to study microscopic evidence.

microscopic—Describing something that is too small to be seen by the unaided eye but large enough to be seen with a microscope or magnifying glass.

ovoid bodies—Oval, heavily pigmented bodies usually found in the hair cortex.

perpetrator—Individual who commits a crime.

physical evidence—Material objects that prove the existence of a fact.

pigment granules—Small particles in a hair that give the hair its color.

pretrial report—A summary of the facts of the case including conclusions based on analysis.

shaft—The strand of a hair that grows outside the body; it does not include the follicle (root).

testimony—Evidence given by a knowledgeable witness, under oath, as compared to evidence from writings and other sources.

trace evidence—Smallest physical pieces of evidence at a scene, including fiber, hair, glass fragments, seeds, dust, and soil, which can only be examined through magnification.

APPENDIX
Science Supply Companies

Most of the materials required for projects in this book are available at local stores. However, certain materials used in forensic investigation, as well as microscopes, are available through science supply companies listed below. Generally your science teacher must purchase chemicals for you. Most companies can be contacted on the Internet; some have online catalogs that will make direct ordering easy.

1 Carolina Biological Supply Company
2700 York Road
Burlington, NC 27215
(800) 334-5551
http://www.carolina.com

2 Connecticut Valley Biological
Supply Company
P.O. Box 326
82 Valley Road
South Hampton, MA 01073
(800) 628-7748
http://www.ctvalleybio.com

3 Fisher Science Education
2000 Park Lane
Pittsburg, PA 15275
(800) 955-1177
http://www.fisheredu.com

4 Flinn Scientific
P.O. Box 219
Batavia, IL 60510-0219
(800) 452-1261
http://www.flinnsci.com

5 Ken-a-Vision
5615 Raytown Road
Kansas City, MO 64133
(800) 627-1953
http://www.ken-a-vision.com

6 Frey Scientific
P.O. Box 8101
100 Paragon Parkway
Mansfield, OH 44903
(800) 225-3739
http://www.freyscientific.com

7 Neo/SCI
100 Aviation Avenue
Rochester, NY 14624
(800) 526-6689
http://www.neosci.com

FURTHER READING

BOOKS

Camenson, Blythe. *Opportunities in Forensic Science Careers.* Chicago: VGM Career Books, 2001.

Conklin, Barbara Gardner, Robert Gardner, and Dennis Shortelle. *Encyclopedia of Forensic Science: A Compendium of Detective Fact and Fiction.* Westport, Conn.: Oryx Press, 2002.

Morgan, Marilyn. *Careers in Criminology.* New York: McGraw-Hill, 2000.

Owen, David. *Police Lab: How Forensic Science Tracks Down and Convicts Criminals.* Buffalo, N.Y.: Firefly Books Ltd., 2002.

Platt, Richard. *Crime Scene: The Ultimate Guide to Forensic Science.* London: Dorling Kindersley, Ltd., 2003.

Rainis, Kenneth G. *Crime-Solving Science Projects: Forensic Science Experiments.* Berkeley Heights, N.J.: Enslow Publishers, Inc., 2000.

———. *Microscope Science Projects and Experiments: Magnifying the Hidden World.* Berkeley Heights, N.J.: Enslow Publishers, Inc., 2003.

Ramsland, Katherine. *The Forensic Science of C.S.I.* San Francisco: Berkley Publishing Group, 2001.

INTERNET ADDRESSES

CourtTV.com. *Forensics in the Classroom.* © 2002. <http://www.courttv.com/forensics_curriculum

Federal Bureau of Investigation. *FBI Youth.* <http://www.fbi.gov/kids/6th12th/6th12th.htm>

INDEX